THE GIFT OF INSTINCT
PARANORMAL LESSONS FOR AN
EXTRAORDINARY WORLD

MORGAN KNUDSEN

For Ansley,
Thank you for all
you do ♡

BEYOND THE FRAY
Publishing

BEYOND THE FRAY

Publishing

CONTENTS

This book is dedicated to all the great minds, in nonphysical and physical, who inspired these lessons. We stand on the shoulders of giants. For Galen: I couldn't be happier to share the cover with you.

And to Chad Lewis: This book is mostly your fault.

FOREWORD

Back in the 1980s and '90s, research into parapsychology was all the rage. Mainstream media continuously covered new and exciting stories of extrasensory perception (ESP), telepathy, out-of-body experiences, remote viewing, and a plethora of other fascinating topics. Parapsychologists and their incredible work were routinely featured on countless talk shows, radio programs, and newspaper articles. Serious parapsychology research was becoming a household interest. Yet, in the last several decades, year after year, I have noticed an appreciable decline in the amount of interest in the same remarkable research that had once dazzled the general public's interest. I believe that this decline is mostly blamed on the inability of scientists and researchers to share the ever-increasing complexity of their research in a manner that makes sense to the everyday person. It seems like modern-day researchers have simply forgotten the most salient question of how this will affect people in their everyday lives. How many times did you sit in your high school math class and think, "When am I ever going to use this stuff?" Unfortunately, the same sentiment applies to dealing with the field of parapsychology. Yes, it may be incredibly interesting, but is it practical?

This is exactly where Morgan Knudsen shines the brightest in her research. Building upon her previous book, *Teaching the Living: From Heartbreak to Happiness in a Haunted Home*, Morgan proves that she is just as much of a rarity in this world as many of the fascinating phenomena she studies. The real-world practicality of Morgan's lessons has set her apart from nearly every researcher on the subject. Her bold willingness to not only push the boundaries of the field, but completely redefine them, proves that the immeasurable praise her work has received is absolutely warranted. The world is full of experts, and as you will soon discover, relatively few possess the ability to convey their knowledge as effortlessly as Morgan.

Morgan is blessed with the unique ability to turn complex scientific theories into the thorough, yet easily digested lessons that form the foundation of this important new work. If you are cynically thinking to yourself that of course it is easy for someone who is naturally "blessed" with a talent to easily excel in life, then you are in exactly the right place. Throughout the book, Morgan expertly demonstrates that we all have numerous abilities lurking directly under the surface; many of us simply need a little guidance in order for these "blessings" to flourish. Nowhere does this ring true more than when Morgan details honing her own abilities while navigating the social perils of high school life.

When I first began reading this book, I was immediately transported back to my days as a young graduate student studying psychology at the University of Wisconsin–Stout. For one of my advanced psychology courses, I lucked out and landed in the class of one of the most remarkable professors whom I have ever encountered. Throughout the semester my cohorts and I sat with mouths agape, flabbergasted by this extraordinary professor. He was the first person I had ever met who was so relaxed, knowledgeable, giving, and self-confident that he appeared to have life completely figured out. To my twenty-something mind, it seemed as though he had been given some miraculous top-secret blueprint to life that the rest of us so badly desired. At the time, I truly believed he had simply been born with the ability to make a chaotic world seem as easily navigable as a quiet neighborhood sidewalk. It wasn't until years later that I realized he wasn't innately "blessed" with these gifts, rather he had worked hard to learn pieces of knowledge that allowed him to spring forward his own dormant gifts. Morgan is following the very same footprints of my professor as she speaks about the importance and self-confidence that come with finding and following your instinct.

Perhaps fate has delivered this book to you. Or maybe you simply followed your internal instinct and decided this is exactly the type of book you need in your life right now. Regardless of how you came upon this work, its life-changing opportunities are now laid out in front of you. In a similar vein to the old *Choose Your Own Adventure* books, exactly which pathways you want to explore is entirely up to you.

Whether it was the chapter lesson on mastering letting go, seeing fear as a gift, or following your own instinct, the true highlight of this book for me comes from the innumerable number of times I found myself saying, "Wow, I had not thought of it like that before." I am absolutely certain that this same thing will occur over and over in your reading as well. Just as I am equally certain that upon finishing this book, you will see Morgan in a similar light that I saw my professor – as the epitome of what it truly means to be a teacher!

Keep an eye out,

Chad Lewis – Researcher of the strange and unusual

INTRODUCTION

In the early 2000s, one of my best friends was going through a pretty rocky breakup. Her common-law boyfriend had wrecked their newly built house, wasn't really working, and emotionally the relationship had taken a nosedive. Finally, my friend had said she'd had enough and told him to leave, which he did, but they continued to message and text, some friendly, some not.

There was something about this breakup early on that raised some internal red flags for me. I say internal because there was nothing on the outside the average Joe would see as an indicator of violence or severe abuse in any way. Hell, I've had worse breakups than this! But I had what I can best describe as an inner knowledge arise in my mind. I say knowledge, not hunch, because it wasn't a guess. It felt as if it had already happened, and I was repeating what I knew for certain. I called her one afternoon and told her what I knew: "Your ex is going to try to kill you. You need to not be home for a couple of weeks."

Needless to say, she thought I was just being an overly concerned friend. She reassured me and said everything was fine, but the information in my head wasn't comforted or resolved in any way. I told her I thought she was wrong but let it go, hoping the seeds of what I said would sink in. A week passed, and I told her again: "You need to leave your house." Again, she told me I was being oversensitive about it, that he wasn't dangerous. I couldn't argue with her because he had never *been* dangerous. I had spent plenty of time with him over the years; I had nothing at all to back up this inner knowing other than a solid and stable understanding that this information was somehow right. This wasn't a guess, and although it seemed like a leap in judgment and theory, for me it felt like the next logical step.

I knew. He was going to kill her.

Finally I sent her an email and was extremely blunt. I told her that I hoped this was not the last time I would speak with her, but that her life was in danger. I told her that he was going to show up at her door and try to kill her, that she shouldn't be home, and that she needed to go stay with her parents for a short time. The nagging feeling that this unknown date was approaching was eating at me. I had nothing to base it on other than pure intuitive knowing. As I wrote the email, I was well aware it may be the last I sent her. I was praying that she would see the light before this came to pass because I knew the proverbial clock was ticking. There was something about him, something about his energy, and something about the overall emotional context of the situation that seemed to be written in the stars. It was as plain as day to me, and I couldn't, for the life of me, understand how no one else saw it. Looking back, there really is no series of steps for many to follow. The people outside looking in likely compared me to Gandalf in *Lord of the Rings* seeing Sauron coming when no one else did.

After sending this email, I got back the response I was dreading but suspected: "It's ok, really. I can handle him."

I knew that was the last I could say in my attempts to be persuasive. I can't recall if I responded or not, but I do remember telling my business partner and best friend, Stephanie Wertz, that we would be getting an unwanted phone call soon.

It was about a week later when my friend called me. I was thankful it was her and not a police officer because the story that ensued was horrifying. Her ex-boyfriend had asked for a ride from one of her family members over to her home. He was carrying a duffel bag and nothing else. He thanked the driver kindly and calmly took the duffel bag from the car and walked across the lawn and up the steps to her front door. He proceeded to push his way inside, open the bag, and pull out a loaded shotgun. "If I can't have you, no one can" was his explanation, and he spoke of how the only way to resolve this was to kill her and then himself.

Unbeknownst to the ex-boyfriend, my friend had brought in a roommate during the time he was gone to help pay the bills, and thankfully, this roommate was upstairs when he heard crazy come in the door. With the ex-boyfriend's back to the staircase, the roommate crept down the stairs behind him and, with extreme stealth and courage, wrestled her ex to the floor and pulled his shotgun from his grip. My friend was able to call 911, and her ex was arrested immediately.

What followed was a lengthy legal process, which I won't

delve into here, and once he was released, he broke multiple restraining orders and finished off his criminal run by threatening the Canadian prime minister, Justin Trudeau, on Twitter. He was subsequently arrested again. As much as I was horrified to hear about what had happened, the news did not come as an unexpected surprise when she called. I was incredibly thankful it did not take a turn for the worse, but seeing as how I had felt like I was watching a car wreck in slow motion for the weeks before, the car crash itself wasn't a shock to me.

This was not my first or my last experience with having information like this on instinct. I knew. This wasn't a hunch, it wasn't a guess: I knew. I knew in the same way you know the sun will rise in the morning and the chair will hold you when you sit on it. It wasn't just that I knew, I was acutely aware of a general timeline. It wasn't some day in the next year: It was now. No argument could sway me from that perspective, and no reassurance could settle it, no matter how logical their arguments appeared.

This was not the first or the last incident where my intuition, my instinct, kicked in. I have a unique ability to see someone I have never met and undoubtedly know that they have a part to play in my journey. Upon talking to who normally would be a complete stranger, I quickly discover that they either feel the same way, or do indeed have a significant role to play going forward. Stephanie was possibly the most memorable for that, as we met in junior high, and as soon as I saw her, I knew we were about to be lifelong friends. She was introverted, in a wheelchair due to her muscular dystrophy, and wasn't actively outgoing or engaging anyone in particular. Months into the school year, we found ourselves sitting out of gym classes in the library at the same table, and we discovered our passion for all things paranormal. We became inseparable, and in 2003, we officially developed Entityseeker Paranormal Research & Teachings. We discovered and developed our unique educational philosophy, Teaching The Living, and soon after, began teaching workshops out of her condo building in Edmonton, Alberta. Within months of that, we landed our first major TV show with Discovery Channel, and the rest is history.

Had I ignored my instinct that she was significant, that she and I were intended (for lack of a better word) to meet, my life story would probably have taken a very different path. Would I be sitting here writing this book? I have no idea, but either way, following that intuitive "knowing" was the best thing I ever did.

There are a lot of fancy words for this in the parapsychology field, the main one being "precognition": the appearance or acquisition of non-inferential information or impressions of the future. Although evidence for things like precognition has been all over the map throughout the years, for me, this and other paranormal phenomenon comes back to one thing: being in close, intimate connection with Who We Really Are. What I mean by that is the nonphysical part of ourselves that we have been taught again and again to ignore and dismiss because communication with it often doesn't manifest physically first. It comes as instinct, as inner knowing, as intuition, precognition, extrasensory perception, psychokinesis, and more. It's the inner connection to the nonphysical part of who we are that puts us, as athletes call it, "in the zone" for paranormal experiences, but also "in the zone" for the rest-of-our-life experiences.

We tend to think that the paranormal is something that happens outside of us and is a rare occurrence. If you see a spirit or have an anomalous experience, then it's once in a lifetime! You were just "lucky." Well, that's simply not true. What's more, the paranormal holds a plethora of insight and lessons, a road map, on how to have more of this inner connection with nonphysical in our lives every day. It's not a once-in-a-lifetime experience, or at least it doesn't have to be! Moreover, the paranormal gives us consistent keys to living in a more connected way.

After twenty years of being immersed in this field, I can tell you that this research does not leave you unaffected or with an unexamined life. If you walk through the world of parapsychology and are not significantly, deeply, and notably changed, you've missed something. In my first book, *Teaching The Living: From Heartbreak to Happiness in a Haunted Home*, I mentioned that parapsychology and the paranormal speaks another language. It's not something that you can always translate using verbal language or equations; it runs the gambit of emotion, sensation, knowing, and reaching a deep part of our internal selves (call it a spirit, soul, inner being) that is crucial to really understanding this work. It is an experience you can't always put on paper, although we need to. It has to be studied and documented and examined. But in this book, I want to share with you some of the deepest lessons nonphysical energy has taught me. Now, everyone's journey is a unique one, and the only thing I can do is impart my small piece of the story. I know my journey is far from done. In fact, I believe it is an eternal one for all of us: we never get it done.

This book is about imparting to you some of the deepest

truths that I've learned throughout my work and journey in this incredible field. These ten lessons aren't really lessons, because you can't really get them wrong, and there's no grade at the end of the day from anyone, physical or nonphysical. I use the word lessons because they are truths that I have uncovered for myself, and they have been lessons for *me*. These are the things that have stuck with me and have been shown to be accurate for me again and again, things I have carried with me in the same way I remember my classes in theater. I don't remember my lines from every script, but I remember universal principles that I now apply to every show and presentation I do. I can't reuse the same script for each new show, but I can remember how vital it is to emotionally impact my audience with what I present to them. I hope these ten lessons have a similar impact for you, because the paranormal has a myriad of things to teach, and very rarely are they showcased in any meaningful way in the mainstream media. Often it is portrayed as the one thing you never want to experience because it might be evil or frightening, when in fact it holds deep information and connection for all of us.

This has nothing to do with religion, although you may see echoes of spiritual teachings here and there. But the paranormal is far beyond the constructs of man-made religious structure: It is infinite in ways we aren't built to wrap our heads around. In this book, I picked the ten lessons I felt the most could benefit from because they are the ten most important to me. I'm certain all of you could probably add five or ten of your own, or they may be entirely different! My hope is, when you read this, that you begin to pay attention to the nonphysical "You" a little more and that you walk away with a broader understanding of the word "paranormal" and the people who have helped shape it, for we stand on the shoulders of giants. We live in an extraordinary world! There is nothing ordinary about this environment, not one thing. We walk through a virtual reality 4D construct that we create daily with our thoughts and expectations: what is normal about that? If someone told you that and you weren't born yet, you'd be saying: "Hell yeah! Let me in on this good stuff!" However, it's dumbed down by what others like to define as "the real world" or "reality," and our hopes are dashed pretty early on in life. "There's no such thing as ghosts and monsters!" our parents tell us.

Well, let's bring some of the magic back, shall we?

LESSON I
TRUST YOUR INSTINCT

"We get messages from the unconscious: dreams, fantasies, intuitions, visions and it is from these that we draw the conclusion of a psychical existence in ourselves which is totally different to our conscious mind. Its psychology is quite different, and the contents which come to us from it differ, in a most peculiar way, from the contents of the conscious. The latter belong to the personality of the ego which is in the world, whereas the unconscious is not, but is rather a world itself. One could almost say it was the world, and that it speaks to us." – Carl Jung, 07/11/1941

I titled this book *The Gift of Instinct* because instinct plays a unique role in our life, and it's often something deemed "unscientific" or just plain silly, when in fact we might not be studying the paranormal without it. Not only does it protect us from danger, but it calls us higher. Now, this is something unique because not every living thing has the second half of that, and just because you're human doesn't mean you've clued in that you have it either. Wikipedia defines instinct as "the inherent inclination of a living organism towards a particular complex behavior, containing both innate and learned elements."

The paranormal teaches us something very interesting, and it is unique to this particular science of parapsychology and quantum physics: you can't take a leap of faith off the diving board of intellectual thought. Sometimes you have to take a leap of faith and then wait for intellect to catch up. The problem with thinking is that it can end up governing too much, and when it does, we lose touch with instinct and our inner knowledge. With parapsychology, often we have to think big and then see if there is any evidence to meet it, and sometimes that evidence comes months, if not decades, later. For example, the idea that vibration played a role in paranormal phenomenon was hypothesized by people like Harry Price, but it wasn't until Victor Tandy that infrasound (a low-frequency sound not detectable by the human ear but rather by bone conduction) was discovered to cause paranoia, hallucinations and other oddities associated with ghosts or spirits. Think about how someone like Harry Price would have felt early on with such a strange notion. There was no real science to back up what he was saying; he likely faced a fair bit of ridicule from his peers and was probably laughed at a good number of times both to his face and behind his back. But his instinct told him differently, and his instinct was *right*. Now, vibration is a necessary word in understanding the paranormal and quantum physics in a myriad of ways, from the smallest particle vibrating at a specific frequency, to the largest oscillating fan causing unwanted physical vibrations in a home and creating infrasound. The initial idea was there, but it didn't start as hardcore fact, it took instinct to lean into the idea that it may be correct and to make the decision to pursue the evidence to support it.

How many times in your life experience have you had the instinct to move in a certain direction? Animals have this innately, although it tends to be for different reasons. They don't rationalize instinct, nor do they stop and question it. In the animal kingdom, you likely don't have time to think about it! If you're a gazelle browsing the African plains for food and your instinct tells you there is a predator in the grasses, you can't afford to waste the time trying to figure out why or how that instinctual knowing arose! You'd better act, or the hesitation could cost you your life! You don't see the gazelle sitting down to contemplate what the other gazelles may think, you move. What's more, the other gazelles who are in tune enough to your motion and your energy will often follow. Have you ever noticed that? When you follow your instinct on something, when it comes from a core or inner "knowing," others matching your level of attunement will follow. The other gazelles may not have had the same "notification" that the predator was lurking, but because they are so in tune with one another, they will leap with the gazelle who does act on their instinct.

Other people know when you are on point with your instinct. It might be only one person, or maybe it's a large group, but others can spot it. Your herd will notice, and when people who are in tune with their own instinct notice you acting from that same centered alignment, there are those who will follow and support you. You'll attract the people who can feel the same knowing you do. They may not know what it is yet, but they innately know it's worth their time, and they may not immediately know why.

Instinct and faith are actually intertwined, and both function best when we don't know the details. Often, when we are put in situations to destabilize us, those are the situations where the most creativity, faith, and instinct kick in. Sometimes knowing too much can throw us off balance because when we know a lot, our filters kick in. The stories we tell ourselves begin to get in the way, and intellect begins to cloud what would otherwise be guidance. If you know everything, there would never be room for instinct, faith, innovation, or discovery. Creativity usually comes in uncertainty, and creativity usually begins with a pinch of instinct. Sometimes you have to shut down your vision in order to have some instinct. Shut down your outer vision and you might just have some inner vision.

In parapsychology, remote viewing experiments are where we see the perfect example of this lesson in action. Remote viewing is an experimental form of ESP (extrasensory perception) that emerged in the late 1960s, in which an individual attempts in a meditative state to visualize the topography of a distant scene or details of an image he/she is not physically privy to. This is a very literal example, but the results have been incredible, even playing a role in the discovery and arrest of criminals such as Saddam Hussein. Perhaps *The Psi Encyclopedia* defines it best as: "*Remote Viewing is the term of art for a series of nonlocal consciousness formalized protocols in which an individual is asked to provide detailed information about a person, place, object, or event, which information they should not be able to know by reason of their being shielded from it by time, space or both."*

The research revealed that remote viewers who were defined as more "right brain," something many associate with artists and emotional thinkers, did better than those defined as "left brain," the more technical or analytical thinkers. Now, this is interesting because, as I stated before, thinking can get in our way. When we are too analytical and allow our thinking to overtake our inner calm, it can blur our connection to that innate ability to hear that deeper part of ourselves that doesn't lean on analytics or reasoning. Women and men did equally well in the research. Often, women are thought of as "more intuitive" or more "connected" because we have an image of intuition being a female trait, but in remote viewing, the ability to receive images, messages and follow their instinct on what they might perceive is equal.

Interestingly, extroverts and introverts developed different strategies for opening to the process of connecting with nonlocal images and phenomenon, and many found that having a ritual of some sort helped with this process. Rituals are often key in slowing down our thinking mind and bringing us into the moment: they empower and connect us. Rituals like meditation and even the act of prayer can be extremely influential in bringing us back in touch with our inner self, as well as setting up our expectations for how the next event or life segment will play out in our life. When we can slow down negative thinking, we can align with far more positive expectations and intentions, which can change the probability of the events we experience.

To illustrate this, the relationship between the monitor and the viewer made a difference, and both affected session outcome. This is such a great example of how our connections to others and how we are feeling can not only shift our experiences, but change our ability to tap into that inner connection. A poor relationship or circumstance, if we aren't mindful of our emotions and allow that negativity to seep in, can alter our chances of perceiving the instinct and guidance we are built to receive. Keep in mind: space and time were not limitations, and no level of blindness had any effect, so this wasn't an experimentation problem. Often the labs used triple-blind studies as the preferable method of research. If the viewers were correct in what they received, and all other avenues to the information had been blocked, they knew the data was genuinely nonlocal and could be treated as a positive result. But mood, expectations, relationships, and environment all played a part in whether or not the viewer could land some home runs, and that tells us a lot about what it takes for us to keep those receptors open! Thankfully, we don't need a lab and triple-blind studies to decide whether or not that guidance and instinct is the real deal, but it can sure help to understand what we're really capable of.

Remote viewing is such a stunning example of instinct calling us higher and having faith that what is being received may be something significant and important, that there is simply more to be learned from the images that people are receiving in this meditative state, and it's not simply a hallucination or imagination. Think about the first individuals who dared to consider that the images in their mind weren't coincidence and that they could receive pictures from people in another room or locations in a far-off land. How crazy do you think they sounded to the average logical person up the street? Throughout history, there have been plenty of cases of prophets and priests and oracles who have claimed to be able to do this. But as time went on, this was considered less and less until now, there is no oracle or visionary who accompanies a president, prime minister or king. It would be considered not only weird, but a practice not based in modern judgment! When all of the medical modern sciences said the opposite, individuals like J. B. Rhine in 1930 decided to follow his instinct and pursue it.

THE LIFE & TIMES OF J. B. RHINE

At the time, parapsychology was still very much a fringe science, and anyone involved was risking their academic reputation. Nonetheless, Joseph Banks Rhine is considered to be the founder of modern parapsychology. An American botanist-turned-psychologist, he was the first to systematically apply experimental investigations in the field of psychical research at Duke University. How does a botanist and someone who gave up a career in ministry because of his scientific beliefs end up the father of parapsychology as we know it? After a stint serving in the army during WWI, Rhine came home to Ohio, got married, and decided he wanted a career change... and he settled on plants. He even when as far as to get a PhD in botany and believed he had found his niche.

In 1922, all of that changed after hearing one lecture. Sir Arthur Conan Doyle was giving a lecture on spiritualism and nonphysical energy, and the list of distinguished scientists about whom he spoke deeply impressed Joseph. Now, remember, this was a man who had questioned his spiritual beliefs in order to pursue a career in what the rest of the world called "science," but something was stirred in him that day. It was further incited by a story from a Chicago professor that caught his attention: he told about a neighbor who had a vision of her brother's suicide, described in detail and verified by several witnesses. Fascinated, he wanted to know more, but the professor seemed to have absolutely no interest in asking why or how this clairvoyance had occurred.

As someone with little belief in any such thing, it would have been easy for Joseph to dismiss both the lecture and the professor's story, but something within him called him further. His instinct told him there was more. This was dangerous territory for someone who worked for a university like West Virginia: This wasn't highly funded subject matter, nor was it respected, but his instinct was to pursue it. Something more called him. He later said: "My interest in psychic research had grown out of my desire, common to thousands of people, I think, to find a satisfactory philosophy of life, one that could be regarded as scientifically sound and yet could answer some of the urgent questions regarding the nature of man and his place in the natural world."

A far cry from a man who wanted to pursue a career in plants!

In 1926, Rhine gave up his job teaching about plant physiology at West Virginia University entirely and decided to follow his instinct. For someone who questioned any idea of religious faith, he had definitely found a new kind! He began training in psychology and philosophy at Harvard in preparation for a career in psychical research. Not many people have the courage to leave their menial job, let alone a teaching position at an accredited university for a position that, at the time, didn't exist. He had no idea if he would ever see a dime from his new endeavor, but that's where faith kicks in. *You can't take a leap of faith off the diving board of logic.* Most people would have thought he was insane! He had no proof of anything he was studying and no job to go to. Even today, we are taught to follow a certain order of life and that any form of uncertainty could land us in a big pot of trouble, especially in the hiring department! Sometimes, however, facts need to catch up to the leap.

My great-great-grandfather, Albert Durrant Watson, was in the same position in the early 1900s. A respected and revered physician, poet, and astronomer, he put his career on the line to tackle parapsychology as well. His career was threatened, he was laughed at, he was publicly ridiculed. However, the instinct and faith were thicker than the naysayers.

Both these men went on to change the face of parapsychology forever, with J. B. Rhine advancing the study of extrasensory perception and founding the Rhine Research Institute. The Parapsychology Laboratory Records at the Rubenstein Library at Duke University contains thousands of letters he wrote during his lifetime. His correspondence with great minds such as Carl Jung, Upton Sinclair, Charlie Chaplin, and Aldous and Julian Huxley, as well as his books and papers, are studied to this day. Albert Durrant Watson involved himself with the Society of Psychical Research of Canada, the first organization of its time in Canada, which pioneered the study of the paranormal in the country, and became president. Having people like Watson and Rhine following their instinct and then having the faith to pursue it, even when there was no evidence, is a crucial reminder of the importance of listening to that inner guidance, and they are far from alone.

Instinct and faith took a career-driven war vet from botanist to one of the most recognized names in science. It took a renowned physician and author to an enlightenment and sense of purpose he never thought possible, and then he changed the minds of Canadians.

I remember being in school and *knowing* that I would not have a regular job. School infuriated me because I knew that nothing I was learning had anything to do with my calling. My instinct, even at an early age, was spot on. In school, because it is one of the few situations in life where we are lumped together with people who are likely not on our wavelength, I was hard-pressed to find anyone whom I felt I truly connected with. It is likely we won't have anything to do with the people in math class ever again, and I would bet ten bucks you don't remember most of your teachers' names or the kid who copied your science homework. I had a deep knowing, possibly the same as my great-great-grandfather's, that I was meant for something more.

When I was fortunate enough to connect with my future business partner, Steph, in junior high, I knew immediately this was the right direction. I had no plans for secondary education, although every adult I spoke to told me it was the only way I would ever see any sort of success at all. My instinct told me differently. Now, let me be clear: This wasn't wishful thinking or a lazy kid talking. Even at a young age, I was a driven writer and performer and spent most of my personal time with my nose buried in paranormal research. I didn't even attend my own prom, as I spent it writing a novel I had been composing that year. But what drove me in that direction was a deep knowledge, an inner knowing, that this was my calling – and the faith to believe I would get there. I had no road map. Parapsychology isn't even a recognized discipline in Canada, so there are no teaching jobs or PhDs to earn. My instinct was simple: if I keep moving in this direction, the door will open *somewhere*. And boy, did it ever.

Now, there is nothing wrong with having a nine-to-five job. There is nothing wrong with working at the local grocery store or bookshop. There is no set plan for anyone, and we all find our joy doing different things. But let me tell you: when you go against your instinct and your calling is to be elsewhere, you can kill yourself by not hearing and validating that inner knowing. And here's the rub most don't consider: you also rob others of your gifts. Like J. B. Rhine, he had no idea he was about to quit his study of plants and become one of the greatest minds in parapsychology. He could have easily ignored that instinct to pursue what it was that really made him lie awake at night and wonder, but what a loss it would have been to all of us who rely on his work as the basis for so many of our theories, ideas and practices now! He could have easily pursued his job as a botany professor and would likely have been extremely successful at it, but nothing got him going like psi research, and his instinct told him to move on it.

Faith played a huge role for me as well, although I never

considered it faith at the time. Instinct has this magical way of making faith look like the next logical step. It feels so natural and so certain that sometimes it doesn't feel like faith at all. Anyone outside looking in, however, might think you're finally going to need that padded truck! And the brazen ones may just tell you so! Faith is the art of believing the unseen is already available to us, and while most people would consider that a ridiculous notion, the truth is that quantum physics would agree that it is not only rational, but extremely probable. In fact, it would argue, you can't have what you can't see in your mind's eye first.

In my first book, *Teaching the Living: From Heartbreak to Happiness in a Haunted Home*, I wrote an entire chapter on probability and how every potential is already in existence and that emotionally "lining up" with those potentials puts you on the same frequency of the event you are seeking, causing it to manifest in its essence. You don't have to see it to know it, but when you're not the one in the driver's seat with the instinct and intuition, others who aren't in your range might see your instinct as something that seems like wishful thinking. A good rule of thumb is this: trailblazers move by instinct. We'll talk about this further in Lesson 10.

NATURAL-BORN INSTINCT

Rock pythons are some of the only snakes that look after their young after they're born. As soon as those little babies hatch and break through their leathery eggs, the first thing they do is turn and go for the grasses and trees. They know instinctually that's where they will thrive: they know the hunting is good there, water is there, shelter is there. What and where do you instinctually head towards? So many times, we are shoved into positions where we could be so much more prosperous had we just followed our instinct, like J. B. Rhine.

If you have the instinct, take it from me, you can hire the intellect. There is nothing I do in my job that I do alone. There are plenty of things I don't know how to do. I don't know how to monetize and market a podcast on a technical level. I have no idea how to tell if the structure in a building is cracked and leaning too far to one side, causing potential noises the owner is mistaking for a haunting. I have no idea how to mix and master the audio that goes into my live shows. But I have the instinct to get these projects going, and the rest of those positions are filled by the people who have an instinct about the things I don't. We have been trained to know HOW to do something, but not the why of it.

I always find it really interesting that even though we keep animals in cages and say they are tame, we still have to lock the cage. Have you ever noticed that? Have you ever asked yourself why? It's because they have the instinct to move towards freedom. It's not in their comfort zone because they may have spent their entire lives in the cage, but let me tell you, animals will exchange safety for freedom almost every time. Instinctually, they know something else is out there. And the reason so many of us are angry today is because we limit ourselves when our instinct tells us "I belong elsewhere." We stay in a job we don't like, in a relationship we hate, or doing something we just don't want to do because we have no background or logical reasoning around how we can get from where we are to what we instinctually *know*. And without that element of faith, you can talk yourself right out of your instinct and make yourself miserable as sin. Just in the same way people can talk themselves into having no ability to remote view or have a paranormal experience by saying, "this isn't real," we can do the same thing with our own intuition around things in our life. Are you working and investing from a *true* place? Or are you working from someone else's expectations?

What are you gifted at? What are you inclined to? What are your passions? Just like J. B. Rhine's plants, if you don't know what your seed is, you can't prosper and grow and bear fruit. You could be wearing yourself out trying to change your environment when in reality, you may just need to change your mind. You can't just discover your seed and walk away, you then have to start to tend to your seed. Now, what seed you bury and nurse is up to you, because you nurse whatever seed you want to. You can nurse a seed of fear, you can nurse a seed of "I'm not enough," you can nurse a seed of "it'll never happen for me," and you can nurse a seed of "I believe this is possible because my instinct is pulling me there." You can pick which one you want to carry and water and dump fertilizer into, and by fertilizer I mean the momentum of more thought. You get to pick, moment by moment, what you do with that instinct and that calling. How you act on it, how you feed it, how you develop it is up to you, and it's your own journey, not your mother's.

Please notice: In the case of J. B. Rhine and other greats of our time, their instinct pulled them forward, but they also had a period of *preparation*. I cannot stress this period of time enough because so often we want everything *right now*. In the case of Rhine, he went to Harvard to prepare himself for his motion forward. Now, not all of us have to go to an Ivy League school, but there are things we can do now to start following our instinct in the right direction.

I used to have a friend who didn't believe in the preparation period. She believed that everything she ever wanted to do she should be able to have and do immediately. Things that would take years of practice, like becoming a musician, she felt she should have instantly and because of that, all my musician friends who had been willing to help her forward with learning the instrument she showed interest in, quit offering their help. She had spoken to me for quite some time about her want to learn drumming and that since she was a child, it was something she had desired to learn. What I found so interesting is that she wanted to be a drummer because drumming requires pace and pace requires a beat, which is something you build on. Yet she was unwilling to find a rhythm and the beat of the drummers who were trying to help her, and ultimately, her unwillingness to learn turned to excuses and eventually made her quit. As far as I know, though I haven't spoken to her in ages, she never picked up the drums again simply because she couldn't master it overnight. She had the instinct that she could drum and that she could play, but her unwillingness to spend time in the preparation period destroyed her ability to follow her instinct. The masters of any craft will not entertain anyone who has the instinct but isn't willing to sit in the preparation period and do the work required. No theatrical performance will hire an actor who hasn't been to rehearsals but has an instinct to sing.

This period is not just in regard to skill, it is also your

energy and emotional center that requires preparation. If you go into a journey believing your instinct to do or be something is the only thing you need, you'll lose whatever you're aiming for in a very short amount of time. It won't be sustainable. This is one of the main reasons so many people win the lottery, and within a short amount of time, they are broke or bankrupt within a few years. In the paranormal world, I see this the most when individuals try to "clear" a house of paranormal phenomenon instead of changing their emotional center so they attract different results. They can stand on their head and do a dance if they want, but if they don't shift their emotional set point, they will continue to re-create the same results they felt they left behind. Instinct is a guiding post, and our work is to follow the signposts and ask ourselves what is required.

You can't make a quantum leap, but the gift of instinct is the gift of recreation. You get the opportunity to recreate who you are and what you are becoming when you follow instinct. No one starts with what they need. You have to develop what you need to sustain you as you bring yourself forward, including developing your core group of supporters.

WHO ARE YOUR MOAIS?

Now, it's important to connect with those we mentioned earlier who share your instinct. These are the people the Japanese call your "moais," your supporters. This is a core group who share your instinct, and it may be a small group. Here's the problem if you try to drag people with you who don't share your instinct: you will drive them crazy.

In my line of work, I find this often because I am a creative, outgoing, high-energy workaholic. I have creativity hit me at all times during the day and night, and that creativity might hit at 10:30. I've sent my co-host of *Supernatural Circumstances*, Mike Browne, text messages at 11:00 at night because I've just had a crazy idea that I want us to develop. Now thankfully, Mike is running on the same instinct, so he doesn't wonder what the hell I'm doing sending him messages when most people are in bed and long finished their nine-to-five. I don't work on a nine-to-five schedule, my creativity never really stops, and the people who do work those regular hours and want to be left alone to vegetate on their couches after five are people whom I can't work closely with. I will drive them mad and eventually they will get angry.

You have to attract the people who will understand your instinct, not drag those around who you *wish* would understand it. You can't make people line up with you; it just doesn't work like that. Please hear me. If they keep a different pace that is right for them, the odds of you changing it without making them want to kill you is next to zero. Don't do it. Like J. B. Rhine and Albert Durrant Watson, your people will find you. They will resonate with you, and it will save you chaos, misunderstandings, arguments, hurt feelings and even sabotage.

Our instincts also evolve; they aren't a static set point in our experience. In the paranormal field, they must evolve because not only are we discovering more about our nonphysical world every single day, we are being bombarded with technology in our life that changes the game. Sometimes we rely on our instincts more than we realize. For example, when I would meet with a client or even another investigator, I would be listening and looking on a multitude of levels. Nuances about dress, their phrasing, the way they tell their story... all of it goes into a database of information both in my head and in my "gut." The joke around my neck of the woods is that you don't dare lie to Morgan: if she asks, she probably already knows the answer, and you'll just end up looking like a fool. I have always had an innate ability to "feel" the truth when someone is talking and put pieces together that don't quite add up. That ability was honed when I was in high school, and because I was bullied, I often had to read the room on a level most other kids never had to. While they were all worrying about the type of nail polish the new girl was wearing, I was reading the room for signs of impending danger or trouble. While it made school a pretty terrible place to be, my instincts now when it comes to energy feeling "off" in a space is deadly accurate. This instinct has also saved my career on numerous occasions, having avoided business deals and partnerships with people who later turned out to be less than trustworthy.

When Covid-19 hit in early 2020, businesses in Canada collapsed. Small businesses were crippled, especially those in nonprofit, theater and entertainment. About a month before it hit, I was doing a photo shoot with a dear friend of mine who owns a production company, and I told him to expand his company elsewhere and dip into live streaming because our province was about to tank. He listened, but I don't think either of us knew what that really meant. I just knew instinctually that both of us had to make some fast and hard changes based on a sudden firing of over fifty-thousand healthcare workers months prior, and every instinct I had told me something was off. A month later, the province and the country was in full lockdown, and we were all out of work. Many entertainers and production companies were left feeling blindsided, and it got worse when the "two weeks to bend the curve" model that the governments had been touting turned into two years and counting. Thankfully, we had already begun to transition, which didn't mean we weren't hurt by it, but nothing after that came as a shock.

Nothing comes "out of the blue." It may seem that way at the time, but if you look back over situations in your life where you felt blindsided, usually you can start to pinpoint subtle signs (or maybe not so subtle) that something was amiss. When Steph and I began delving into the paranormal and investigating cases, instinct was what caused us to create our specialized program, Teaching the Living. We began to notice behavior patterns, not just with our clients, but with the spirits we were interacting with. We started to see a direct correlation between the client's emotional state of being in the world and the activity they were getting back spiritually. We would see some extreme cases where clients would tell us, "This attack just came out of the blue!" but when we looked back on what had happened prior to the aggression, we began to see behavioral indicators that lined up with one another over and over again. We began to notice that the client was in a certain emotional fluster, or there was a prior "warning" from the entity before the onset of aggression. The problem came when the person was so out of touch with their own instinct, and therefore the correlation of their behavior to the reaction, that they kept repeating the same mistakes and couldn't see they were a contributing factor.

I can't tell you how many clients I have dealt with over the years who have told me, "I knew something was off when I moved in," or, "Something didn't feel right, but I ignored it..." and the rest is history. Ignoring our instincts, whether it be with an aggressor we can't see or one we can, can carry a price tag most of us aren't willing to pay. Sometimes it's physical, emotional, financial, or all of the above. Our instincts are in place to guide us, and when it comes to the paranormal, sometimes that's all we've got. One thing I have found with entities, good and bad, is that conversation with them happens on a variety of levels. Verbal communication is not usually the first on the list. We speak, act, and present with our energy, which is seen first. Animals work this way as well. You can say the nicest things in the world to a dog that's growling, but unless you present with the right calm-assertive energy, the dog is going to hear a bunch of nonsense coming out of your mouth. Spirits are often the same way. It's not that speaking isn't used; it's just not used *first*. Believe it or not, many *people* are the same way, and you may be one of them whether you know it or not.

Our intentions rely on our instinct. In order to use your experience, your education, your gifts to any benefit, you have to be in touch with your instincts. This is one of the number one lessons I have learned from mediums over the years, people who are extremely plugged in to their instincts in regard to nonphysical anomalous phenomena and messages. You can go to school, get the degree, get the education, apply for the right jobs, and have everything right on paper, but have no instinct to execute when it comes to timing, speaking, or acting. When we have such intellectual prowess, sometimes we can lose that instinct, and without it, our intentions falter. As an investigator or paranormal researcher, you can buy the gear, get the team, have a logo, and go to all the locations you want, but if you are out of touch with instinct, you're going to get tired of this pretty quickly. You'll spend a lot of time setting up all your expensive toys, waiting around, and tearing it down again only to hope for the best at the next place. Even those who work mostly in the parapsychology labs such as PEAR (Princeton Engineering Anomalies Research) work with instinct.

Instinct is often the hunch that inspires an experiment or fuels an idea. Without it, breakthroughs wouldn't come nearly as often as they do, and the parapsychology and scientific community wouldn't be anywhere close to where it is today! Quantum physics, something the parapsychological science is quite tied to, is often driven by instinct and hunches before evidence is ever discovered. Inspired ideas driven by the instinct that there are *more* discoveries like the Higgs boson, discoveries like this that change the fundamentals of our understanding of the universe. If we did not have the instinct to expand, we wouldn't even bother with the question to begin with! Just as we learned with J. B. Rhine, a question, followed by intention and fuelled by instinct, can change the course of your life, and the course of an entire field of influence!

LESSON 2
MASTER LETTING GO

"The greatest illusion is that mankind has limitations."
– Robert Monroe

This could possibly be the most difficult lesson to convey to others, mostly because of our indoctrination that "working hard" and being tough is a virtue of great success. Working *hard* and acting *hard* means you will be incredibly successful, and if you aren't, you simply aren't working *hard* enough. When we look at the results in society, we know that is a fundamentally flawed principle. There are plenty of hardworking people in many lines of work who can barely make ends meet at the end of the month, and even more who seem to move from one bad relationship to another like it was clockwork. By the same token, I know just as many people who have wanted and hoped and pushed for a paranormal experience or visit from a loved one and still can't seem to experience what they are seeking, or what they have experienced is so terrifying they would rather forget it. What, if anything, do these things have to do with one another, and can the paranormal give us a hint as to why these issues persist? The more we want, the harder we work at it, the less we often get, and the worse it can spiral. *Why?*

When Steph and I first started out in the field of paranormal research, we were pretty limited. We were young, didn't have a whole ton of money, and transportation was limited due to Steph's muscular dystrophy. Our minds, however, knew no bounds. EVP (electronic voice phenomenon) was one of the first things we dove into because it was something that we could study without having to go to faraway places or invest a lot of cash we didn't have. We would quiet a room, whether it be a place we knew or a place we were called in to investigate, and we'd lower the lights to lessen distraction, get super serious, and start asking a long list of questions, trying to entice some otherworldly presence to have a chat with us. I look back on these early (and fun) moments and laugh now, because twenty years later, my outlook is quite a bit different. But back then, with far less information, we really felt we knew what we were doing! We experimented with cassette tapes and digital audio, various microphones, cameras, and all sorts of various gear, trying to record the coolest thing possible.

Now, don't get me wrong, we had a couple of doozies. The most notable came from an abandoned hospital in Edmonton, Alberta, where we recorded a blood-chilling scream, which we caught on both audio and video recorders, as well as heard by three investigators. It was a fantastic display of what's known

24

as "residual energy," a recording of audio in an environment thought to be caused by high levels of electromagnetics and cellular memory. However, more often than not, we recorded absolutely nothing. Hours and hours of audio were deleted because there was just nothing there, and we began to realize that something was missing in our approach. We were working hard, we were putting the hours in (oh boy, were we ever!), we asked and left target objects (objects we would encourage the entity to move in hopes of communication), and then asked some more. Nothing. Zero.

I'm honestly not sure when the turning point happened, or if it was just something we noticed happening gradually, but when we connected the dots, it changed *everything*. When we were getting results, whether it was objects moving or EVPs or other interesting physical phenomenon, it was during times of us just hanging out and having fun. It wasn't in the moments when we were being stoic and serious; in fact those were the times we could almost guarantee nothing would go on at all. The events were happening when we had almost forgotten why we were sitting there and had gone off on a completely different topic altogether! We would be covering all sorts of subjects: bad jokes, creative ideas, or a fun memory! It didn't really matter as long as it was making us happy. Once we began to the play the recordings back, we would catch all sorts of fun things: footsteps, voices, laughing, conversations, and some-times appropriate responses to what we were talking about. We never did a serious EVP session ever again!

THE STUDY OF LETTING GO

This experience was later confirmed to us through a rarely talked about but incredibly important study done in Ontario, Canada, known as the Philip Experiment. I wrote about this extensively in *Teaching the Living: From Heartbreak to Happiness in a Haunted Home*, so I won't delve too deeply here. But in short, the experiment consisted of members of the Toronto Society of Psychical Research and MENSA coming together and discovering that responses and psychokinetic reactions to questions and séance-type sittings were only manifested when the groups let go of their seriousness and began to have some fun. The consciousness they wanted to speak with wasn't actually a real person at all, but rather a character named Philip whom they had fabricated entirely. The energy and focus they plugged into believing that this "person" had once been alive was so intense, they manifested a consciousness from thought alone. However, it only responded and the experiment only took off when they added in fun and began chatting about other things around the table rather than trying to fight something into existence by "battling it out."

This notion follows suit statistically with paranormal experiences in general: the more distracted you are from the idea of having a paranormal experience, the more likely it is that you'll have something happen, like seeing an apparition. Throughout years of research, parapsychologists have seen the results again and again that people who "let go" and are doing some kind of mundane task where their mind wanders or they are in some form of meditation will tend to have a paranormal experience before someone who is intensely focused on it. Those who have less attachment to the idea will generally have something happen before those who are trying hard to "make it happen." Psi awareness, or that perfect state of consciousness where you have a good chance at experiencing some kind of anomalous phenomenon, is said to occur at a certain stage in meditation attainment. It is an aspect of the greater sensitivity and awareness that follows from removing the noise of the internal dialogue. In the 1970s, William Braud introduced the psi-conducive state, related to meditation, where he states that psi functioning is enhanced when there is a combination of:

- cortical arousal sufficient to maintain conscious awareness
- muscular relaxation
- reduction of sensory input
- internal attention

Now, this all sounds technical and sciencey, but really it comes down to this: cool things happen when we let go and chill out. That's it. There are a lot of really great books studying all sorts of neuroscience and parapsychology and epic biographies on meditation masters, but at the end of the day, the message is the same: chill out and let go. In 1990, Braud took a hard look at the studies in regard to meditation and psychokinesis (or PK, the process of influencing our physical reality with our thought and focus). An analysis of all such studies reported between 1971 and 1988 found that seven out of eight meditation practitioners at some point showed a stronger PK effect when told to influence the numbers of random number generators.

Now this is all pretty small stuff in the minds of most

people, but it really isn't. What we are coming to understand in the world of parapsychology is that letting go and taking the pressure off is the key to everything we really want. Not just altering numbers of a random number generator in a lab, or generating a thinking entity we created on paper, but in regard to our overall happiness and success as well. You want to change your results in life? Letting go of the fight might be your first step, and often letting go takes its shape in the disguise of forgiveness.

BE SELFISH: FORGIVE

Unforgiveness and the inability to let go becomes baggage that can hold up your potential, your instinct, your income, your dreams, and your connection with nonphysical. Think about it like being at an airport: When you check in, the employee at the desk asks you about your bags. How many are you checking? She also checks the weight of each bag, and if you're over the weight limit the airline allows, it starts to cost you. Sometimes you're even told you can't bring it on the plane at all! If you're over the weight limit, it becomes a barrier to your travel. You can't get where you want to go if you're bringing too much with you, and if you don't let go of it, you won't even be leaving the ground! The airline will turn you around at the door and sell your seat to someone else who has less baggage and is prepared for the journey. See how this works?

When most people read an idea like this, all of their old patterns tend to come to the surface in the form of "but I can't."

You probably had a whole bunch pop into your head right now: "But I can't quit my job!" or, "But I can't let go of that grudge; you should have seen what they did!" The list of "but I can't" is endless; you could probably write a list a mile long because most people can. Our instinct is to gravitate towards happiness, but our list of reasons why we can't do that beats us down before we can even get out of the gate. Instinct cannot operate on "but I can't," and letting go of the struggle is one of those key steps to moving forward that society struggles to quantify.

Glorifying the fight is one thing we are really good at, especially in the West. All of our heroes have struggled a long time, and despite all odds, they reached success on some level. "If you're not struggling, it's not worth your time" and "if something is worth keeping, it has to be hard to get" are common philosophies we hear from parents and teachers alike. Whether it be a struggle in the workplace, in relationships, or to have an experience we so desperately want, it is drilled into us at an early age that the harder you push, the more likely you are to get what you want. In other areas of our life such as relationships, "don't forget what they did to you!" or "if I let go of what they did, then it makes it ok!" are other forms the "but I can't" mentality infiltrates our instinct. The big problem we all face with this mentality is that, at the end of the day, it will still cause you to miss your plane! The attendants of your journey will still pick the person who is prepared for the ride, and if you are rooted in pain, anger, bitterness and resentment, it will be clear you aren't yet available for the experience.

Almost nothing in the world teaches us about the pitfalls of baggage and not letting go more than negative hauntings. These are the hauntings where the entity involved will manipulate, hit, bite, scratch and generally cause mayhem in a home or business. Steph and I spent a long time in our early days studying these unique and occasionally frightening thought forms because we found their behavior and relationships to people fascinating. The more emotional baggage people were carrying, the more likely one of these new buddies were likely to be there, and they are almost always a reflection of the dominant negative luggage the person is hauling around. One of the most interesting things we found throughout our studies was this: Negative entities can be indicators of unforgiveness. These thought forms, which appear to be emotion that has festered long enough that it has become conscious and independent of the thinker, often stem from the living's inability to let go.

Baggage comes in many forms, but it is our own thinking that ultimately gets in our way. It comes back to the same thing that experiments like remote viewing begin to show us: when our mind is cluttered, so are our emotions, and our visions ultimately take a hit because of that. When you rehearse those visions and images in your mind, you enshrine them, and then they manifest as the *essence* of that energy in our experience. We often think we're hiding these old wounds from others, but it becomes impossible. People might not know the details, but our behavior, our actions, and our energetic point of attraction will radiate messages we aren't even aware we're emanating. Negative entities become indicators of emotional turmoil because emotions we stuff down never stay buried – that energy must go somewhere and often expresses itself through phenomena like psychokinesis: the manifestation of our emotions and focus in our physical space.

Forgiveness is saying, "what affected me is not stronger

than me," and letting it go is not allowing it to take control of your destiny. Forgiveness and letting go is about disconnecting your tether from the baggage keeping you grounded, not about justifying what injustice may have been done. The problem with "being tough" and hanging on to what you're angry with is that the price is huge: the price is looking out the airport window as plane after plane of opportunity, relationships, peace, and adventure head for the runway without you. You'll be standing at the window of your gate, wondering and feeling frustrated that you didn't get the break you were looking for, or another person left you, or you can't seem to get a leg up. Or, in the case of many, why you've got negative paranormal experiences following you from place to place. It's all the same energy, and it's all intertwined: it is just a manifestation of negative emotion, baggage you haul around that might include negative expectations, a negative self-dialogue, unhealed fear or hurt, or something toxic you haven't been willing to release yet.

Women can be the worst for this because we are taught from a very early age to "be tough." If we forgive what has been done to us, then we are giving permission for it to happen again. The reality is it takes far more courage to forgive than it does to hang on. Forgive can be read as "fore give love," and it really has very little to do with the perpetrator of the injustice or the situation.

For me, the case that comes to mind was a young woman whom I consulted with in 2018. Her story had all the hallmarks of a horror movie: Her family was sleeping in their car because they were living in fear of the entity in their home. It had attacked their son and her, and the only one it had even a twinge of respect for was her husband. The thought form ran the house and controlled when they went to bed, what they did, how they did it, and was physically violent towards the young woman in particular.

When I'm taking cases like this, the target person is always of interest to me for a number of reasons. The one who is being attacked or assaulted usually holds the key to the entity's behavior, and if you want to know why that person has been chosen as a punching bag, you just need to take a look at what the entity is doing. It is almost always a direct reflection of the open wound the living person is carrying around.

Initially, when I asked her about her past history, she gave me the rose-colored glasses version, which almost everyone does. Everything is perfect, my family is perfect, my life is perfect, and there is no reason for any of this! Fix it! But when you begin to ask a few more questions and get people comfortable enough to share their story, the story that doesn't look as good on a magazine cover, the activity becomes far less of a mystery. In this case, the woman had escaped a physically abusive relationship with a past partner. She and her son had made it out by the skin of their teeth and, thankfully, met a new man (her current husband) who was everything she had wanted. She had moved on but never forgave or healed the situation, and the emotions she had were left festering.

See, others will often reflect our wounds back to us, and we get angry that they seem to be acting crazy! The paranormal is such a stellar example of this because it is so unbiased. It is such a pure energetic reflection of where we are in our hearts and minds, which is something most people don't like to hear. It's easier when the activity is being afflicted on us than it is to take ownership of our role in the process. In a case like I just described, the long-term solution becomes healing our own issues so that we can present a new vision, new energy, and new frequency in our environment. When we radiate differently and are dragging less luggage around the airport of life, suddenly all those gates that were once closed to us start to offer us some first-class seats! In the same spirit, the anomalous phenomenon begins to shift as well. This is the essence of my program, Teaching the Living, but it applies to every area of our experience.

Letting go not only opens doors for us, but it allows us to connect with the instinct to act when the time is right. When we are no longer distracted by pain and anger, our instincts heighten automatically. We feel things we simply could not feel before because the pain was in the way. It hinders our receptivity to opportunity in the physical world and connection with the nonphysical part of ourselves, as well as consciousness as a whole. All of those hints and nudges from the Universe go unheard and unheeded when we're wrapped up in hate or our thoughts are occupied with whatever argument we just had on Facebook. Even though the anger might seem justified, we have to remember that it doesn't come without a price tag. Just as Steph and I found out through EVP and the SPR discovered during the Philip Experiment, that connection gets lost the less fun we're having. The more we let go, the better it gets.

Think of how hard it is to drag huge bags around the airport or around a shopping mall. Think of the effort it takes to keep up with the normal pace of the crowd when you're hauling that much stuff – speed isn't even an option! You can't keep up that race for long distances, and let me tell you, life is a marathon, not a sprint. There is a limit to your energy: mental, emotional, and even physical. You can only go in so many directions and carry so much before the engine begins to break down. When you've got split focus due to not letting go of what's not needed, not only does it cut us off from our instinct, but it stops us from keeping up with the momentum and pace the Universe moves to. Nonphysical energy has a pace and a beat, and it operates best when we are in joy. When we are able to drop that baggage, our hands become free to cheer and say, "Hey, pick me! I'm ready! I'm open to what's in store! I'm ready for these experiences! Bring 'em on!" This is where making peace with where you are becomes so important.

Part of forgiveness is about letting go of changing the past. Rehearsing what has happened in your mind holds you hostage to the energy that is now disrupting your current experience. No matter what we are doing, our power resides in this Now moment, because every future moment will be a Now as well. We really can't ever escape the current moment; it is always Now, no matter what. One of the great gifts that the paranormal gives us is the practice that our power is in our immediate experience: when we change our outlook, the outlook changes. When we practice choosing joy and letting go, no matter how you do it, you shift the numbers on your "random number generator" of your experience. You change the outcome and influence the matter and circumstances around you. The more joy you find, the better your experiences are with nonphysical energy and the spirits you encounter. The phenomenon begins to reflect the healing you're doing, and the letting go creates space. Read that again.

Letting go creates the space for your new experiences.

ROBERT MONROE & THE GATEWAY PROJECT

In 1958, Robert Monroe had an experience that would change his life.

Robert was born in Kentucky and had a number of pursuits, which included music, drama, trains, cars and aircraft. He didn't grow up indoctrinated into religion, and despite taking pre-med courses at Ohio State College, he switched to mechanical engineering, then proceeded to drop out by the time he was seventeen. Robert became a runaway kid, of sorts, and began living the life of a street person and hobo, hitching rides on trains and with strangers and taking odd jobs. For a short time he was a newspaper reporter but left that too, feeling like it was not what he was meant to be doing. I'm sure by the time he was in his mid-teens, no parent on the planet felt he would amount to much apart from being a directionless kid on the path to a life of silly dreams and reckless behavior.

After a year of wandering, he returned to Lexington and re-entered college, becoming a radio host and opening a theater company. The arts, he discovered, were a passion, and before long he was offered a job he felt drawn to: a radio writer in Cleveland and then again in Cincinnati, where he was offered yet a third job with NBC's show *Rocky Gordon*. It paid so well, he did the only thing he could think of with that kind of money: he bought his first airplane by the time he was twenty-five. His calling and passion drew him to yet *another* job, and he was hired by the National Aeronautic Association to produce a weekly radio show on aviation.

By the 1940s and '50s, Robert had become a name in radio;

he produced shows such as *Take a Number* and *Name That Tune* and purchased numerous radio stations. But even more importantly, his passion led him to an unexpected road: he became an innovator in sound technology, being one of the first to use magnetic tape. However, it wasn't until 1958 when his life changed forever that he stepped into something he did not expect.

In the spring of that year while sitting and meditating, Robert experienced a sudden cramp in his side that he couldn't shake. Weeks later during another meditation, he found himself paralyzed, unable to move. His body shook fiercely with no explanation, and once he felt that was over, a sensation of warm light poured over him and through him, which he could not explain. Over the next six weeks, Robert had this happen again and again. Instinct told him not to fight the phenomenon, but to let go and see what happened next. Several months later during another experience and keeping in his awareness the conscious decision to let go and surrender, he pushed his fingers down into the bed to find that he was now touching the floor. As he pushed harder, he felt more of the floor as if his fingers and hands had sunk into the house itself. The next time it happened, he reported something new: he was looking down at himself in his bed, asleep next to his wife.

Robert was excited, and with this new knowledge and formula of meditation and surrender, he began to control his movements while he was floating, verifying his locations and venturing further than he had before. In the 1960s, Robert lost two friends, and instead of worrying about their deaths, he decided to try to speak to them while in his newfound nonre-

THE GIFT OF INSTINCT

sistant out-of-body state. Within a short time, he saw both deceased friends and spoke with one of them.

After a brief period of research with Charles Tart, Robert was inspired to create his own laboratory where he could unleash his ideas and study with no constraints. Having experimented with "sleep-learning" through aural stimulus during sleep, Robert was determined to find an audio signal or sound that would allow listeners to let go and stimulate out-of-body experiences at the same time. He tried for some time with no success, but eventually one of his scientists read about an idea: binaural beats, sound fluctuations that result when two slightly different tones are heard in each ear. Inspired, the team created audiotapes with binaural beats at the low frequencies that correspond to brainwave frequency at altered states of consciousness. When each hemisphere of the brain synchronized, they began to experience positive results of OBEs.

Knowing he had discovered something incredible, Monroe sold off his last remaining radio stations to follow his passion. He threw all his time and attention into what he called "hemi-sync technology" and, in 1975, received his first patent. He developed a program people could participate in, which he called "the Gateway Project," which began with a mere forty interested and eager participants. In 1977, Robert left his tiny lab and found a larger property, which he developed into the Monroe Institute, a place where all those who wished to study his endeavors could congregate.

Robert began attracting people who were on point with his purpose, including Joe McMoneagle, a leading "remote viewer" in the Stargate program, an elite operative program with the military specializing in remote viewing. Joe participated in a

Gateway course in 1982, finding that it improved his preparation time for remote viewing and made his results far more
accurate.

Robert's life was not without tribulations, however, and in
1983, Joe married Robert's stepdaughter, Lea. He was in high
hopes for the relationship, and Lea became the director of the
Monroe Institute until 1991, when he and Lea had a devastating
falling-out. In 1992, Robert's wife passed away, and in turmoil,
he attempted an out-of-body experience to find her. So upset
and disappointed he was by his failed attempt, Robert gave up
on participating in the OBEs himself. With his mental and
physical health deteriorating from the estrangement from his
stepdaughter, Robert knew he had to make a choice. His
depression was manifesting as illness, and he reached out to
reconnect with Lea, who reciprocated. At age seventy-nine,
having made peace with Lea, he passed away in 1995.

Biographer Bayard Stockton described Monroe's life as a
pragmatic approach by which "he helped to de-mystify what
others refer to as the occult, the supernatural or supernormal,
even the metaphysical, for many other people... the introduc-
tion of a potent new technology in some branches of medicine,
in education... and, conceivably, in business... his tools-of-the-
mind may be far more useful than has heretofore been
suspected."

Robert's OBE experiences were so profoundly prolific and
impactful, they can only be best described in his books, as
summarizing them would do them a terrible injustice. Monroe
never delved into the idea of reincarnation or the soul, but felt
that life after death was nearly a certainty after having commu-
nicated with many spirits while experiencing his OBEs. Now he

touches lives still with his videos, programs, and the legacy of the Monroe Institute, which is carried on by Nancy McMoneagle and is furthered today by researchers like Allyn Evans and Joe Gallenberger, whom I will speak about later in this book. However, his most impactful legacy may be in fact the thousands of people whom he reassured, the people who had been experiencing psychic phenomenon and were labeled as "mentally ill" or "crazy" by medical science. Sometimes, hope and direction can come from the strangest places, including a wayward kid dropping out of school and hopping trains, following his instinct, and being brave enough to let go.

So take a look at the bags you have packed up beside you. As in *The Matrix*, this is a red pill/blue pill moment. Do you want to create more of what you have, or do you have some things you need to let go in order to experience the new adventure? The paranormal reminds us to take a look at our bags, unpack a little, and survey the inventory. Only then can we check our bags, buckle up, and hit the runway knowing we're ready for the next adventure.

LESSON 3
FEAR IS A GIFT...AND A MIND-KILLER

Most of us nerds know the Litany of Fear from Frank Herbert's famous novel series, Dune. According to the Dune Fandom Wiki, it was written for "a person whose nature is still primarily bestial, recoils from pain and seeks to flee it to preserve itself, a person of higher nature goes through it and out the other side in order to remove the threat permanently." In the world of the paranormal, the word fear is something people often think of when they talk about strange phenomenon, even though statistically the majority of people experience uplifting occurrences. There is, however, a sliver of the population whose experiences have been frightening and sometimes outright horrifying. Whether we delve into the world of hauntings, UFOs, or cryptids, experiences can be life changing in the worst ways as well as the best.

After twenty years of being immersed in these cases and working with individuals as well as myself, the world of parapsychology has taught me a fair amount about fear, and at times, it has been trial by fire. With fear, there is little room for practice outside the practical. Unless you've got your hands buried in it and your legs knee-deep in the mire, exercising experience with fear is almost impossible. It's one of those things that can't be taught out of a textbook or in a lab, it has to be in your face, and you need to be neck-deep in it before you can really discover what fear has to teach. Everyone's lesson with fear is different, and I want to impart to you what I've learned in my own journey in hopes it may help you in yours.

The fear of the unknown is a fear that encompasses nearly every person on the planet. For centuries, we have used everything we can to try to put explanations to the unknown: folklore, legend, religion, and of course science. These have all played a role in soothing our fears of what might be around the dark corners, even when the explanation may not be entirely correct.

We've also developed rituals and ceremonies to help us pace ourselves through our fears. Many cultures believe crystals or herbs will cure their home of evil spirits, hanging a horseshoe on the doorway facing downwards is said to ward off witches, or putting brick dust across an entryway could mean your enemies can't set foot in your space. There are endless things humans have come up with to ease the fear of what might be "out there" and to explain away unknown happenings.

Sometimes we come across a scientific explanation for that unknown thing, and even that doesn't dissuade people from continuing with the ritual if the fear still lingers. Seeking a sense of control is something that people gravitate towards under any and all circumstances. It's one of the reasons psychics become so popular! They temporarily ease the ambiguity of our futures when we don't understand that it is we who are creating the next moment, not some external force. But when things feel out of control in our lives and fear starts to take over, people stop listening to fear and insist on fighting against it. When that happens, all meaning goes out the window, and the lesson or the message gets lost.

TWO TYPES OF FEAR

A question I get asked frequently at both my shows and interviews is "Do you ever get scared when you're doing this kind of work?" That's always a loaded question for me because the answer isn't as simple as the interviewers want it to be! One thing I have learned in this field is that when it comes down to it, there really are two types of fear: learned fear and instinctual fear. First, let's talk about learned fear. Believe me, the two are very different even though it may seem like I'm splitting hairs or playing semantics. Learned fear comes from the thoughts we think about a situation, person, or subject, and those thoughts can come from a myriad of places.

I am up close and personal with people who have this type of fear often because I have a python. People are not innately afraid of snakes, despite what many believe. I grew up having no fear of snakes whatsoever, or of any reptile for that matter. In fact, I gravitated to them because their lack of fur and feathers was encouraging for someone like me who suffers from a fair number of environmental allergies like dander! I've had a variety of reptiles my entire life and have come across a plethora of people who are afraid of them and those who love them as much as I do. One thing I found when I've spoken to those with a phobia is that their fear usually comes from a false narrative or incorrect beliefs about the animal, and often these were learned from their parents or close family. Chances are, if you had a parent afraid of snakes or spiders, you probably are too. After correcting many of the false ideas about snakes and exposing people to pythons like Galen (who would prefer to help decorate the Christmas tree and play in the park than scare anyone), many people begin to rewrite their narrative about snakes and realize their beliefs and the story they had written around the idea that snakes are horrible was simply not true. New experiences replace the old ones, and their emotions begin to shift towards a far more positive outlook! This is learned fear, and often it just takes some self-examination to understand what is actually causing it. It also takes a willingness to be wrong and to question what we tell ourselves.

In relationship to the paranormal, this is all too common. What's worse, we tend to create what we fear on a couple of levels: both behaviorally and vibrationally. What we fear we attract, because whenever we have high levels of any type of emotion, by the nature of quantum physics, we draw to us more of whatever is vibrating at the same frequency of our being. If we're in fear or we are telling a fearful story, guess what? You'll inevitably recreate the same circumstances to justify your position. There is nowhere this is a more teachable moment than in parapsychology, because hauntings and psychokinetic activity are so intensely governed by our emotions and state of being. When we walk into a haunted location and have already told ourselves a story of how frightening it is, how spooky, how dangerous, or how terrible it might be, we are setting ourselves up for the Universe to deliver exactly what we're worrying about.

We live in an inclusive universe, and we include things by use of our attention. When we are placing our attention on what we are witnessing or on thoughts we might be thinking, we activate those thoughts as a potential probability in our experience. How different would the Philip Experiment have gone if the sitters had come at it from a place of fear? What would Philip have been like? Would "he" have been violent or aggressive? One thing is for sure: when we focus on negative paranormal activity and pay it our attention, it becomes more. When it comes to a paranormal event, fear is an emotional indicator, and it tells us to stop and re-evaluate how we're thinking about a situation. The major difference between learned fear and instinctual fear is that learned fear often stems from judgment. If you ever get stuck on trying to figure out the difference, that's the best way to figure it out. Is there a reason you don't like whatever this fearful thing is, or is there a barrier to how you're thinking about it? Fear is how you test your thinking: how you speak, how you understand and how you think. Is there something happening in your thinking or how you're being that is creating the reality or the fear that you're teaching yourself? Have you challenged how you're thinking? What if your thinking, your speaking or your understanding *isn't working*?

Often, people who vehemently believe that anything para-normal or spiritual is evil run into this problem. Incidentally, I find that people who have negated all evidence of anomalous phenomena as fake fall into the same mental trap. Learned fear will collapse your learning every time. Read that again: learned fear will collapse your ability to learn. This is where instinctual fear differs from learned fear in a big way.

Instinctual fear causes you to become aware, it focuses you into the moment and opens up your senses. With instinctual fear, you automatically begin to take in new information. You become aware of sights, smells, and noises that you were hardly noticing before that instinct began to kick in. It's the instinctual knowing and alertness that causes the antelope to immediately take notice of the downdraft scent of the leopard prowling nearby. It's also the fear that tips off a woman who suddenly realizes that the blind date she's now on isn't going to end well if she doesn't figure out a way to exit carefully. It's also the same fear my clients often describe when they've entered a haunted place and things just feel "off." I can't tell you how many times that phrase has been told to me during interviews or how many times I've felt it myself. Fear is an opportunity to turn inwards and ask ourselves the hard questions, and often this requires us to be the observer of the fear: be in it and not of it.

Instinctual fear will save your life. I like to call it connected fear. Connected fear is when you are in tune enough with your mind and with your inner self that you pay attention to the subtle (and sometimes not so subtle) gut-level information that your body and your being is feeding to you all day, every day. Connected fear can come from a few places and often includes lessons learned and stored in prior situations. Our brains and bodies gather data, and that data cumulates in a variety of ways. As I mentioned in lesson 1, instinct can derive from past experiences: incidents that have taught us valuable lessons and have given us the ability to see red flags coming. But when we're connected to who we are at a deeper level than simply telling ourselves a narrative about that which we are not challenging in a more profound way, we begin to read the situation, person or experience from a place of inner knowing rather than the story we're feeding ourselves. This connected fear doesn't require us to have a previous frightening experience either. Sometimes it can be a brand-new experience and our proverbial warning bells still sound.

THE MURDERS & LESSONS OF JAMES WATSON

On my walking classroom, Historically Haunted in Edmonton, Alberta, I repeat a story about Edmonton's first (and possibly worst) serial killer, James Bluebeard Watson. You might be thinking "What does this have to do with the paranormal?" Let me tell you: your instincts don't simply play a role in a haunted place.

James Watson resided at a historical (allegedly haunted) apartment building, which has since burned to the ground a few times; however, his legacy survived. He murdered nine of his victims at the Arlington apartments, all women whom he persuaded into a long-term relationship and marriage. He would prey on women, ask them to marry him, and then find some horrific way to kill them and dump their corpse wherever it suited him.

Watson originated in America but was chased up to Canada on bookkeeping charges and was, by then, a suspected killer. He hopped across the country, settling in various places until making himself comfortable at the Arlington under his latest alias. He had so many aliases that the police never did find out his true name and sentenced him under the James Watson pseudonym once he was finally arrested. It was only later they discovered his true name, Charles Gilliam, and that he was born in Arkansas in 1870. Carl Sifakis, in *The Encyclopedia of American Crime*, credits Watson with forty-odd marriages and "at least twenty-five" murders, but Watson's own confession was somewhat more modest, listing nineteen wives and seven murder victims.

He described that his crimes felt like an impulse, a momentary outburst, which he could occasionally, but rarely, resist. He told police that sometimes he could resist the temptation to kill the wife he was with, and in other times he would execute them in whatever fashion he felt like in the moment. He "accidentally" pushed one from a boat, bludgeoned another with a hammer, yet another with a rock, and threw one over a waterfall while on vacation. A month later, another nude body was found outside town, strangled, her skull crushed, and breasts and genitals slashed with a knife.

Interestingly, the key to Watson's undoing lay in one woman's connected fear. In the spring of 1920, wife nineteen had a strange feeling about her new husband. She had no obvious reason to think ill of him because on the surface, he was an outgoing man she hadn't thought twice about marrying at the time, but an inkling of fear told her something wasn't right. Now this young woman ended up hiring a private investigator, citing the reason that she believed he was cheating on her. However, as a woman, I have always felt that she suspected something a bit more. A cheating husband is one thing, it's a whole other when you hire a private investigator behind his back and don't confront him yourself. Something told her it wasn't a good idea to approach him with her suspicions, and she couldn't have been more right. Most wives would be standing on the porch, waiting for their man to come home or snooping through his things for evidence of infidelity, but something told her deep in her gut that she needn't be the one to directly confront her husband.

The private investigator ended up finding two bags upon searching Watson's belongings: one full of wedding rings and the other, marriage licenses, all of which were mementos from his prior murders. Even the private investigator knew that this was far beyond his pay grade and notified the police immediately. Watson was arrested and extradited back to San Quentin, where he plead guilty to murder and was subsequently given a life sentence.

The Arlington apartment buildings, or rather the empty lot where they once stood, has now become notorious for strange black shadows moving amidst the grounds and rubble. When it was still standing, the Arlington building frustrated police, as they were often called to investigate potential squatters. Lights and fires were seen in the windows, and when police would secure the premises, they would either end up chasing out unknown shadows or see people in the windows who turned out to be nonexistent. It was suspected that arson finally finished the building off in the early 2000s.

Now think about this case for a moment. It would be easy to label this young woman as simply a jealous wife, but because we know about James Watson and his horrendous crimes, we can look back and realize much more was at stake here. It's too bad we can't go back in time and interview his wife to find out exactly how she was feeling before she decided to make that call to the private eye, but present-day women who have been in similar situations can give us some clues to what she may have been thinking and feeling at the time. Even though we can't get in her head now, we can examine her actions and come to some conclusions about what she may have been going through. Her actions undoubtedly saved both her life and the lives of countless other women. Had she not called a private investigator and been brave enough to hold her secret while he investigated, she likely wouldn't have lived to share her suspicions with anyone else. Something told her there was danger around the corner, even though she had no direct evidence of what it might be. It would have been easy for her to talk herself out of her feelings by saying "this is my husband" or "he couldn't possibly do anything to hurt me" or "I'm so angry, I'll confront him anyways," but she chose a different path, and it ended up saving her life. It would be interesting to know how many of Watson's victims felt the same inkling that something wasn't quite right with him and told themselves to stuff their instinct, as so many of us do today.

Connected fear is our inner self throwing us warning bells that we need to pay attention inwards and that something has entered into our experience that requires us to become aware. Ultimately, connected fear is the presence of something that disagrees with our inner being – and our inner being is calibrated to joy. The more we align with our natural state of being, the easier it becomes for us to interpret these signals and to tell the difference between learned fear and connected fear. Now you can see why I hate the question "are you ever afraid in haunted places?" It's a long answer, but an important one. For me, the short answer is no. I have learned to be the observer of the emotion of fear and don't get lost in it; I am also conscious of my own internal dialogue. My expectations when I go into a haunted location are usually quite positive, and while I've had some interesting encounters with entities over the years, I don't feel fear around them. That wasn't always the case, as I remember being a child and having a strong mix of both fear and intense curiosity around these types of anomalies, but the dialogue I had with myself played a key role in shifting what was left of that fear and moving it into fascination.

I was really good at developing a relationship with fear at an early age, and it's something we all must do. Fear isn't going away, and we don't want it to. It is an opportunity and a teacher of insight, presence, and an indicator that something crucial needs to change. That change could be a long-held belief, a life pattern, or an immediate situation. Fear is a call to action both internal and external. We all have a relationship with our fears, but we often forget that we are in the driver's seat of those relationships, whether it be with connected fear or learned fear. If we carry too much of it with us, it is bound to get too heavy. The paranormal teaches us to be logical in illogical situations, and fear can do the same thing, but in order to do that, we need to pay attention to the relationship dynamics we have going on. When you have a healthy relationship, you have healthy boundaries, and fear needs boundaries. You cannot have a good connection with fear until you develop boundaries. I've dealt with clients who are so terrified of the haunting in their home that they are sleeping in hotel rooms, but by the same token I have met people who are so frightened of becoming ill they have not left their home or seen a live person in over two years. If you're not careful, fear will kill your dreams if you let it. Whether it be that house you scrimped and saved for that turned out to be filled with weird phenomena or the business you wanted to start and gave up on, fear will chop the head off of whatever you've got going on if you're not careful.

Mastering our fear and learning to listen to it is a balance. It's an intricate dance, and I spoke about it in my book *Teaching the Living: From Heartbreak to Happiness in a Haunted Home* when I talked about my relationship with fire. As a fire performer, respecting fire is crucial. It is never something you master, it is something you dance with. It is a partner, and that partner can still have bad days. It has a mind of its own, and any fire artist will tell you the same thing if they have a mind to do so! In the same way I have learned to interact with the powerful element of fire and do so without fear, the paranormal can be very similar. It teaches us to change fearing the unknown into embracing the unknown, accepting it for all its pitfalls, crazy moments, inspiring ideas, thrilling rides, and heart-stopping moments.

One of the worst things we can do is try to suppress or stamp fear out without the awareness of why it's there. Byron Katie once said, "If you argue against reality, you will suffer," and what she meant by this is that our present moment is always here to tell us where we are so we can get to where we want to be. When we are pushing against "what is," it will always cause "what is" to perpetuate. Accepting "what is" does not mean "what is" is ok or that you've given up, but if you continue to deny or push down whatever the reality is that you're experiencing, it will prolong the suffering. Continuing to deny an instinct or feeling of fear, whichever kind you feel that you're experiencing, will only drag it out longer, and it will grow. I can't stress that enough. If you continue to ignore the scary in your house, in your job or in your relationship, whether it is a haunting or a cheating spouse, it's going to get worse not better. Accepting it, not necessarily liking it, will open up the opportunity for you to choose how you are going to respond to it. Until you acknowledge the fear, you will close that door of opportunity and negate your responsibility in whatever is going on.

Learned fear, if we are not managing it, will leave us susceptible to predators because it cuts off our awareness, and we can end up stuck in our heads rather than in our gut. We tend to believe ourselves, so if we are telling ourselves the wrong thing, then we can end up walking into the mouth of a predator and convince ourselves we're just fine. It will overrule connected fear if we're not careful. Connected fear will keep us safe if we allow it. When we are disconnected from the experience, we will miss what the Universe and our inner self are trying to tell us.

In my experience, the most effective tool in any haunting, as well as within fear-driven situations in our own lives, is love. It sounds like a cheap answer, but I'll tell you, it *is* the answer. Think about what your reaction would be to a learned fear such as another culture you might not understand or an animal you've never experienced before if you approached the situation from love and curiosity rather than your own biased dialogue of beliefs? Changing fear to curiosity comes from a place of compassion and openness. In the lab, parapsychology studies *must* come from a place of diverse open thinking because if it did not, our approaches would end up limited. Our fear would break the flow of inspiration and keep us in a narrow box of interpretation, something the scientific community has been known to struggle with.

Parapsychology teaches us to live with fear but walk by faith. We must do the work, we must experiment, and we must work with science to move the field in the right direction; however, without the faith that there is indeed something more to our current understanding, we're going to be doing a short sprint rather than running a marathon. We want the marathon! The marathon is where we learn the skills and develop our understanding and relationships with emotions and instinct, like fear. Without the marathon, we miss out on key pieces of the journey, and in doing so, we won't sustain our place at the finish line. We train differently for a marathon than we do a sprint. We prepare our endurance, we prep ourselves mentally, we work our bodies in a new way, and we know that it isn't going to be a success-only journey. We know that there are going to be moments when we slow down, moments where we're fearful, and moments when we feel like giving up. How much of that marathon do you think is run in the mind before it is ever run on the track?

∿

FEAR NOT

The biggest lesson on fear the paranormal has taught me

has been one that has surprised most people, and that is "fear not."

Fear not.

The wonderful thing about parapsychology is that you cannot walk through it without coming to the inevitable understanding that we have authority over our lives in a way that has never been thought possible before. All of life is for us, nothing is against us, and everything is temporary, even on a particle level. We are eternal beings, and we really do have everything we need; no one can give us anything we don't already have. Fear not. I can unequivocally say that my understanding and my relationship with fear has been positively changed for the better because of the paranormal. Even though it is easy to get wrapped up in the television shows that want to create jump scares and horror stories, you'll find that delving into parapsychology properly will be the greatest journey you will ever embark on, and when you come out the other side, you'll find your experience with fear has become quite different. You will discover that you are a timeless being who is meant to bring the eternal qualities *into* time. Things such as innovation, creativeness, and resourcefulness are all flowing, and you have an abundance of access to all of that information and knowledge. Everything, even fear, will pass.

Have you ever noticed that there is no source of darkness? In parapsychology the study of light is paramount to what we do. Everything is light: how we perceive our world comes down to light energy and how our eyes and brains translate it. Nothing moves at the speed of darkness. There is something in parapsychology known as extraordinary light phenomenon: the experience of a seeing an extraordinary light, quite different from ordinary physical light, seems to be a rare but universal human experience. It is described as brighter, stronger, and more intense than anything else known to humankind. It is more radiant than natural light, appears in various forms and shapes, and is sometimes perceived as an autonomous entity that can perceive, think and act. Some people feel communication with it; others feel like they have been guided or experience encompassing warmth. For most people, this is a life-altering experience, and the presence of this nonphysical light confirms a belief in some sort of continuation of consciousness beyond death, which is said to be one of the top fears of people today.

Strangely, the paranormal dispels fear far more than it invokes, something most don't consider when they think of ghosts and things that go bump in the night. But the reality is the paranormal generally shifts people's lives for the better, and those who have experiences report a reduction in fear and anxiety rather than an increase. The paranormal calls us forward as beings on this planet and lifts us past the understanding that we are meat suits walking around with a finite purpose. Often, the fear for many people derives from the idea that the ego must let go of old paradigms and belief systems. The fear of changing our perception of the world is often far more daunting and terrifying than the idea there is anomalous phenomena.

Fear drives people into pushback. There are few topics as controversial as life after death, survival research, or hauntings. Fear can also drive a solid wedge into conversation and families if it is not navigated properly. One of the areas where fear presents the biggest challenge in hauntings is between parent and child, when the child is experiencing activity or has intuitive or mediumship abilities and the parent has never dealt with something like that before. I have watched fear drive parents like this to bribe their children to keep quiet, punish them for having the experience, or even shun them for being fearful so they don't have to deal with their own relationship with fear. When people are forced to come face-to-face with fear, all skills and even parenting abilities will and can fly out the window if we aren't monitoring our emotions. Again, the paranormal forces us to be logical about the illogical, and when we mix fear in the middle, it can be a hot mess fairly quickly. Raising a child is complicated enough, and when you encounter something as far out as this phenomenon can feel, parents will often reach for any tool they can to try to quash the issue entirely, and sometimes those tools can do more harm than good. We have to be careful when we are reacting in fear towards others because what can happen is that we begin to blame the other for our own faulty relationship with the fear itself. We blame the other person for having an experience that doesn't fit within our realm of physical understanding, and they become the one at fault. When it comes to children, they have a unique ability to make things their fault anyways, and parents can drive that home by accident if their own relationship with fear isn't healthy or examined.

The paranormal is like a check and balance when it comes to the subject of fear, and without it, we struggle as people to expand our horizons and think outside the box. Embracing the unknown and letting go of fear becomes part of the tuning in process. In lesson 2, we talked about letting go, and it couldn't be more relevant than now. The paranormal, the supernatural, elevates us to a new level of understanding of who we are the amount of power we have in our reality. Sometimes this is good and bad, depending on what your reality currently happens to be! But acknowledging it gives us the opportunity to grow into that power. The hardest fights are trying to fight the intangible, and that is ultimately what fear really is. Conceptual exists only in the creative realm, and fighting for stuff from a place of fear of lack tends to be easier to get our minds around. It's very difficult to point a finger at something nonphysical and blame it when you can't put your finger on it, and here presents the challenge. If you don't feel safe in your head, you can't be creative, and creation is always in the realm of nonphysical. There is no alternative other than to rise above it. Creative energy, Source energy, is hard to recognize when you're in the middle of a storm, and often people get so frozen in the fear of the answer, the result is they do nothing. But here's the problem: If you are stuck in the middle of mediocrity, you won't step up to the opportunity or new level of thinking that will carry you forward. Parapsychology challenges us to say goodbye to our old ways of thinking in order to get to the level you are coming into.

WHAT WOULD YOU DO IF YOU HAD NO FEAR?

Whatever your answer is, that is what your fear is robbing from you. You can't delve into parapsychology without faith, in the same way you can't advance yourself to your next arena without faith. When you have that connection with Who You Really Are, your inner being, you can walk above fear. It's only the ego, the home of the learned fear, that will walk you right back under water. When that becomes conscious, you'll sink. There is nothing about the paranormal that teaches us to crawl, it is all about flying and soaring. When you're flying, you need to get above the high winds because if you don't, you're going to have some turbulence.

What people don't realize is that everything they want begins as emotion first. Thought creates, and thoughts are attracted to us through our emotional state, not the other way around. Many will tell you that we simply can't help but think a certain way, but quantum physics shows us differently: everything begins as nonphysical first. Every idea, every thought form, every emotion all starts as energy. Everyone wants the physical manifestation, and when you live in the grips of fear, you cut off the instinct and creative connection to the Universe that will propel you to where you want to go. You will never be rid of fear, nor do you want to be, but having that healthy relationship and boundaries is going to make or break how you think and feel moving forward, and therefore affect what you attract. You can deliver greatness, but we can't do that if we are breathing the air of toxic conditions like debilitating fear. It causes our perception to change. The filters we are looking through change when we are in flight or fight, and we can read into issues and problems that may otherwise not be there.

Fear is a mentor. Failure is a mentor. Not all mentors are teachers or even people! If you're not willing to fail, then you're not willing to be a part of the process. I can almost promise you that I have failed more times than you have eaten breakfast! Where the difference lies between those who have worked through and succeeded and those who haven't is rooted in their beliefs and relationship with fear and lack. Remember: we create what we fear, every time. Whether it be paranormal activity or a job that scares the dickens out of us, owning our fear means we get to respond. We get to choose. At the end of the day, we get to look fear in the face and ask the question: if you had no fear, what would you do?

LESSON 4
YOUR DEAD LOVED ONES AREN'T
STUCK...YOU ARE

In about 500 BC, the philosopher Parmenides spoke of light as a symbol for both truth and being, as did Plato and Plotinus, as well as Bishop Gregory of Nyssa. In many other cultures, a guiding or white light is mentioned as well: the "pure" light of the Upanishads in India, the Buddhist's "white light," and the light of illumination and enlightenment in the Jewish, Christian, and Mystic traditions. What's interesting is that no matter what culture you skip to, paranormal phenomena such as lights, out-of-body or near-death experiences, hauntings and psychokinesis are almost always present. They are described in a myriad of ways, but they are often, if not always, central to many belief systems.

Probably one of the most popular themes in today's world of ghost hunting is the drama of our dead loved ones being stuck, unaware they have died, and desperately need the help of a special psychic or medium to "cross them over." This didn't start with television, believe me, and although parapsychology finds quite the opposite, the concept of the human soul possessing a light-filled core is common to folk traditions, and that core needing to be somehow "crossed over" using human means is also not new. In some Christian religions, it was common that the church must be paid a sum of money in order to get a loved one out of purgatory and into heaven; and in Ethiopia the Zar possession was a popular affliction and could only be resolved by paying an exorcist to remove the alleged evil spirit from the victim. Interestingly, the victims often consisted of women not obeying their husbands, and what became known as the Zar Possession Strategy began to occur, where the women would act possessed in order to force their disagreeable husband to pay a financial price for their annoying behavior.

"Many think success means getting everything I want. And we say, that's what dead is, and there is no such thing as that kind of dead. Success is not being done; not being complete. Success is still dreaming and feeling positive in the unfolding."
~ *Abraham, channeled by Esther Hicks*

The fear of the dead coming back to haunt us or even kill us has been a fright that lasts to this day, or the fear of a loved one becoming stuck on earth and unable to transition to a new nonphysical reality has often played a role in our thoughts about death. It always surprises people when I tell them that there is no existing evidence in parapsychology or survival research to support these claims. As far back as survival research goes, even the best minds in the world from Princeton, Edinburgh, and Yale have found no evidence that this is the case at all. However, the living are another story altogether. If the paranormal has taught me anything throughout the years, it is this: our loved ones aren't stuck, *we* are. And "stuck" looks like a number of different things depending on the individual.

Those who have scientifically worked with mediums, such as the Windbridge Institute in Tucson, Arizona, have reported back consistently themed messages under double- and triple-blind studies, and that is "We are free and we are joy. You are loved. Come join us!"

It's not the belabored mourning sadness that we've come to expect from Hollywood spirits or horror films, but it is the message that is consistently delivered again and again through the best channelers under study and those who have had near-death experiences (NDEs).

THE GIRL ON THE BUTTERFLY WING

Perhaps one of the most significant experiences of our time was that of Dr. Eben Alexander, a neurosurgeon and brain researcher who underwent a near-death experience in 2008 during a coma caused by bacterial meningitis. His account of his NDE during the time he was unconscious sent a shock wave through the parapsychological and scientific communities because not only was his experience remarkable, he was a neurosurgeon and a man of science. This wasn't a layman misinterpreting a dream, this was a man who brought both education and reputation to the table, and he was willing to put it all on the line to tell his story.

For a long seven days, the entire neocortex of Eben's brain, which rules higher functions such as language and logic, was nonfunctional. At first, doctors believed that it was a strain of *E. coli* that carried the threat of further spread, but upon further inspection, it was not. In fact, the doctors had never seen a case like this before and estimated his survival around ten percent. It didn't look good. Bacterial meningitis, especially with the severity to put someone in a coma, was usually considered a death sentence if there was no recovery within a few days, and despite pumping him full of every medicine they could think of, Eben's response to each one was poor. At best, the doctors anticipated that if he ever woke up, he would need care and have speech problems for the rest of his life.

On the seventh day, the doctors approached the family with the news no one ever wants to hear about their loved one: maybe it's time to stop treatment. However, it was just the words his son, Bond, needed to make one last effort. He ran into his dad's room and begged him to wake up, and to everyone's surprise, Eben did just that. He opened his eyes and began choking on the breathing tube, which was promptly removed. Immediately he looked at his family calmly and said, "Thank you. All is well." Unbeknownst to his family, this was just the beginning.

After two months of recovery, Eben began to recount something that changed his life. While he was in the coma, he had an extraordinary experience that began with losing all sense of space and time and falling into darkness, losing his body, identity, memory and language. His consciousness was clear, but it was attached to nothing, and he described himself as simply a point of awareness. He later referred to this state as the "earthworm's-eye view."

After a period of time in this state, Eben noticed an object of brilliant light that began to spin and rotate, emitting beautiful fragments of gold and white as it spun and broadcast a lovely song. He later called this the Spinning Melody. As he gazed upon it, he began to realize he was gazing through it, and as he did, his vision opened up to a luscious country plain of green grass, rushing streams, waterfalls and joyful people. Eben later called this place the Gateway. As he watched it, he began to fly across it, gliding effortlessly, and as he did so, a girl appeared beside him. She was soaring on millions of radiant colors, what he described as similar to the colors of a butterfly wing. The Girl on the Butterfly Wing, as Eben now calls her, had a message for him that was clear and resounding: "You are loved and cherished, dearly, forever. You have nothing to fear. There is nothing you can do wrong."

As he continued to soar through pink-tinted clouds and up even higher, he noticed he was also soaring with bright, shining orbs of light. They zipped about him, darting this way and that, and he instinctively knew these were intelligent beings, wiser and far older than he. His senses, like sight and hearing, were not separate here, and everything blended together in a cacophony of light and sound. Each time he had a question, answers appeared instantly and easily, like an explosion of love and wisdom. Everything he ever wanted to know was accessible, and there was no time between the question and receiving the answer. Eben then described arriving at an infinite void, or Core, which was dark yet full of light at the same time. What he experienced there would take a lifetime to unpack and understand, as he stated. Information flowed to him and through him, and he was able to recount only a fraction of it: that there is not one universe but many, with many forms of life; that loves lies at the center of all of them; and that although evil exists – including on Earth, because there is free will – it is relatively rare.

Throughout his time there, he traveled between the Spinning Melody, the Core and the Gateway repeatedly, and he found that what drove his movement was his intention, not physical action. He played and journeyed through this expansive universe for ages until he tried to return to the Gateway again and couldn't get in. He was devastated, and his intuition told him the experience was coming to an end. He heard beings talking to him and saying uplifting things to keep his vibration high and happy, and he began to see faces of people he knew were important to him here on this planet. Eben began to feel himself losing touch with this realm, but the beings instructed him that this new reality was always with him. "My mind – my real self – was squeezing its way back into the all too tight and limiting suit of physical existence, with its spatiotemporal bounds, its linear thought, and its limitation to verbal communication," he writes.

While many people keep their awareness of their physical identity during an NDE, Alexander did not, and he believed it was what allowed him to go further without any attachment to expectation. He went on to author a book about his experience entitled *Proof of Heaven: A Neurosurgeon's Journey Into the Afterlife.*

When asked about his experience, Eben wrote: "Our truest, deepest self is completely free. It is not crippled or compromised by past actions or concerned with identity or status." It is a sentiment that I have experienced working with hundreds

of haunted places as well, and it has been followed up by channelers such as Esther Hicks (Abraham), Louis Benjamin (the
Humble Ones), and Jane Roberts (Seth). What I have found
most often when I am dealing with the living is that we have a
tendency to get hung up in the "what is" of our emotions. Grief
is one of the most difficult emotions to move through, and
we've been taught that the longer we hang on to grief, the more
we must have loved that person. The worse we feel, the more
love we must have had. It's a terrible premise, but one most of
us grew up with. As soon as people saw someone having a
glimmer of positive emotion around the idea of death, that
person would be shunned as someone who was simply not
caring.

Cultural roots play a part as well, and in many cultures, the
spirits of the dead are simply seen as evil or in some belief
systems, they simply don't exist altogether. Within the world
and science of parapsychology, things are much different. Eben
Alexander is not the only one to report these kinds of consistent, life-changing experiences upon death or coma, and he has
not been the last.

Although one thing had Eben troubled: unlike many NDE
reporters, he had not seen any loved ones he recognized. A hall-
mark of near-death experiences has often been the report of
seeing loved ones in shape and form that they are recognizable,
and he had seen no one but the Girl on the Butterfly Wing. His
father, who had died a few months earlier, didn't seem to be
there, and he began to doubt his experience entirely. His questions lingered until, one day, he received a photograph that
sent his world reeling again. It was an old photo of a young girl,
his biological sister Betsy, who had passed away before he ever

got the chance to meet her. He was stunned to see the face in the photo was none other than the beautiful Girl on the Butterfly Wing. In that moment, he said, his conflict was healed. The worlds he lived in, which included fatherhood, his medical practice, his relationships and his magnificent experience, became one, and his doubts about the nonphysical aspect of who we are and who we become were no more.

What I have found in haunted places mirrors Dr. Alexander's sentiments completely. One of the things that I am asked often is "How do I talk to my loved one now that they have passed over?" and usually these same people come to me with an empty pocketbook, having paid all their money to psychics who have promised answers. Or they have simply been told the spirit of their loved one is "stuck" on earth and there is no way for them to move on until they reach some sort of emotional closure or they are pushed along by the living.

My lesson from this nonphysical plane has been: the energy that creates worlds doesn't need human action to do what it does so naturally. As humans, we put limits on this vastness that people like Eben Alexander describe that are simply unrealistic and only serve to make ourselves feel more involved in the process. But the reality is it is not our process to be involved in, and everything really is well and taken care of. Many reports of hauntings and spirits who have presented themselves to loved ones more often come with the same type of message that Eben received from the Girl on the Butterfly Wing: "I am ok. You are loved." This is not uncommon despite the horror tales we like to watch on television, and the accounts of negative entities are another genre of paranormal activity entirely, not upset people lost and disconnected from who they really

THE GIFT OF INSTINCT

are. The reality is the evidence is overwhelming in favor of a nonphysical world that is flourishing, full of love and well-being, the epicenter of knowledge and thought, and the Core of everything we have ever imagined and beyond. The well-being that abounds here is hard for us living people to truly wrap our heads around, and perhaps we aren't supposed to quite yet, but we can get glimpses of it through the experiences of people who have slipped into nonphysical through things like NDEs or processes much less dramatic like meditation. In simple processes like calming our minds, finding joy, and other such practices, speaking and reaching the consciousness that is nonphysical (and our loved ones who are now there) is actually quite simple. The challenge is ourselves.

What I have come to understand is that the spirits we long to talk to become pure positive energy once they lose the weight and ego of the physical body. The pain, both mental and emotional, is left far behind, and the living are stuck with memories of a grumpy old man or nasty old woman who might have had a very different persona while they were alive. What we are shown in parapsychology is that those embodiments of personality do not stay with the being who has moved on, but rather a far more positive and uplifted version of the person remains. The study of personality surviving death is an ongoing one, but the parts that seem to survive are the parts that are closest to who they now are: joy. Often the living people seeking to reach out to a loved one who had a rough person-ality while they were physical can find them unrecognizable upon making contact with them either through a certified medium or through their own interactions. It leaves family members doubting the experience altogether because ornery

Great-Aunt Mabel is now a joyful, playful and caring intelligence that wasn't at all like the woman whom they remember! This can leave some pretty hefty challenges for the living, especially when they have their own emotional scars to heal if they were close to an individual like this. They are left with the damage while the person they knew has moved well beyond that, and a new relationship can be established. We all like to think these nasty people we've encountered will be dealt some horrible punishment in the afterlife... however there is simply no evidence to support that.

So what do we do?

The Universe calls us forward. There is no backwards. And the way to connect with that which these people now are, this nonphysical energy, is to resonate with the joy in which they now exist. As the channeled personality of Abraham once said through Esther Hicks: "Lighthouses don't go running all over an island looking for boats to save! They just stand there shining!"

In my program Teaching The Living, I talk extensively about how we tune into nonphysical like a radio dial with our emotions broadcasting the frequency we want to be on. When people are in grief, that is often when they want to talk to their loved one the most, and it is about the furthest from the right "radio station" you can get. This, in my mind, is one of the reasons people who reach out to nonphysical in fear and grief often end up duped or attacked by an energy that simply isn't very friendly, a thought form resonating in the same dark emotion that those people have their dial at. Usually, right after a death is not the time to be attempting communication. Interestingly, the people who are in grief and have an experience with a nonphysical loved one are usually in a place of no emotional resistance. Sometimes they can be doing the dishes, vacuuming, or doing something where they can let their mind wander and their grief subside. That's why meditation is such a great practice for these times when emotion gets the better of us: it stops negative thought and gets the door open a crack to let in what you're asking for.

Here's the great thing about the Universe: It is always calling us to joy, every time and no exception. There is no dark switch, only our own ability to cut ourselves off from that Core that Dr. Alexander described. One of the reasons that Eben may have had the experience he did was that, in a coma, you really are in a place of nonresistance. Any negative momentum you had going in regard to your healing stops entirely, and you let go in a far more complete way. He wasn't listening to the doctors tell the family he barely had a chance, that the medication wasn't working, he was probably going to die, and all the other messages of despair his family was being delivered. In the end, being stuck means that our connection to the source of who we are is impeded by negative thought that we pick up along the way in our physical life experience. Once that is let go through the death process, "stuck" is not possible. The Universe is always calling us to more. Inexplicable healings are not uncommon after a person reports an NDE, along with increased intuition or even psychic abilities, such as precognition and telepathy.

In 1977, a gathering of interested professionals and experiencers led to the founding of the Association for the Scientific Study of Near-Death Phenomena. Four years later this organization became the International Association of Near-Death

Studies (IANDS). It often surprises people when they discover that the individuals heading organizations and research like this are also physicians like Dr. Alexander. Those people have included but aren't limited to Raymond Moody, medical sociologist John Audette, social psychologist Kenneth Ring, cardiologist Michael Sabom, and psychiatrist Bruce Greyson. Although Raymond Moody had published his work on the matter, *Life After Life*, it was not considered scientific research by today's standard.

Kenneth Ring, professor of psychology at the University of Connecticut, set out to provide a substantial scientific foundational basis for NDEs, introducing satisfactory sampling procedures and comparison groups and quantifying variables. To measure the NDE experience, Ring constructed the Weighted Core Experience Index (WCEI), components laid out by Moody in his book, and they interviewed over one hundred people who had claimed to have an NDE. They investigated the incidence of NDEs, whether NDEs are influenced by the circumstances that cause them, and the possible influence of religious beliefs as well as NDEs that occurred along with suicide attempts. They even went further and investigated what life changes occurred after the experience was over and how the people were affected long term. Despite a few minor differences, Ring's work supported Moody's, and it was the beginning of a substantial scientific platform to continue work on near-death experiences and survival research.

Bruce Greyson, former professor of psychiatry at the University of Virginia, has made a substantial contribution to NDE research over the past thirty years and has composed over one hundred papers and scientific studies in medical, psychological, and academic journals in support of what people like Eben Alexander have claimed. He also created the Greyson Scale, as he conceptualized the NDE as a set of factors that were cognitive, affective, paranormal and transcendental. In his conclusions, he states, "The real challenge of explanatory models of NDEs lies in examining how complex consciousness, including thinking, sensory perception, and memory, can occur under conditions in which current physiological models of mind deem it impossible." Regardless, NDEs remain one of the best glimpses we have as living beings into the transitional experience of the death process.

Another notable who lends his skill and study to this subject is British neurophysiologist and neuropsychiatrist Peter Fenwick, who has researched NDEs since the 1980s. Educated at Trinity College, Cambridge, Fenwick is now a visiting lecturer at King's College, London. He has run a neuropsychiatry unit at the Institute of Psychiatry, London, and specialized in epilepsy. Fenwick continues to be president of the Scientific and Medical Network and the Horizon Research Foundation and has authored books on the subject of NDEs and how they have shaped the lives of those who have experienced them.

Another project known as AWARE launched in 2008 and involved a total of fifteen hospitals in the UK, USA and Austria. Its findings were released in 2014, and over a period of four years, 2,060 patients suffered cardiac arrest in the participating hospitals. Among the 330 who survived, 140 were considered eligible for the program and were interviewed. Fifty-five had memories of the time they were unconscious, and nine (6%) had memories consistent with an NDE. Of the two patients who had detailed memory as well as audio and visual experiences within the event, one had verified accuracy of events while the other had unverified accuracy of events. It is significant that verified memories were recalled during a time when the patient was unconscious and in cardiac arrest.

What makes these studies so interesting is that it may show us a glimpse into the afterlife that may not be available to anyone outside of actually dying! And it is consistent with visitations by spirits in haunted homes when the spirit is felt to be of human origin. The key is: we don't need to have a life crisis to tune in to these energies! All it requires is a little more patience and a lot more caring about how we feel and our own joy. These experiences beg us to ask the question "are you up to speed with your own Core?" Or has Who You Really Are as a joyful, energetic, passionate being become lost to your own version of "stuck"?

The other area of "stuck" people tend to misunderstand is their own perpetuation of beliefs. Remember, we create our reality through our focus, and if we indeed are focusing on the same thoughts of lack every day, our reality is changing, but it is simply changing into the same set of circumstances again and again. Until we have the awareness and discipline to get our thoughts out in front of our current circumstances, we doom ourselves to create a repeat of the same until some life-altering event happens or we get sick and tired enough of our circumstances to change it. Humans really do have to get to the point where they are sick and tired of being sick and tired before they really make any changes that have the potential to stick long term.

Nonphysical, the Universe, our Core, is ever flowing and always moving, but how we move with it is up to us. Are you putting your canoe in the river downstream and going with the flow, or are you jumping in and paddling harder than ever trying to get upstream? Like Eben Alexander discovered: everything you want is downstream and ordered by your intention. If your self-dialogue is "I'm never going to get out of this job," or "I'll never see better times," the Universe will happily deliver. What we think and what we manifest is always a vibrational match, no exception. So when we want an answer from nonphysical energy, do you think the answer is in the vibration of the problem or the vibration of the solution? Where are you putting your attention?

Paying attention is the most valuable currency you have available to you.

Your attention will keep you stuck, or it will create magic. It will bring you hope and wisdom, or it will hold you in the darkest places. It will bring incredible relationships with your deceased loved ones, or it will hold you apart from them. Make no mistake: they are calling you forward, all day. What you want and what you dream about is calling you forward; life is a never-ending unfolding that is coming forth through you as long as you allow it. Our glimpse into the energy that creates worlds and the messages we document from the certified mediums, such as those from the Windbridge Institute or the Forever Family Foundation, offer us guiding posts to find the core of who we are so that we can connect with them in the realm of nonphysical energy. Whether we go or not is up to us.

Parapsychology and the paranormal have also provided research into yet another lesson: the paranormal can bring us *out* of being stuck just as our thoughts can get us there. A great example of this is the work of Dr. Callum Cooper of

Northampton University, who specializes in thanatology, the study of the social and psychological effects of death. For Cooper, his work goes even deeper than that and into the realm of bereavement and the effect of anomalous experiences on the bereavement process. Cooper argues that anomalous experiences actually help people through the grieving process, and further research has shown that those who reported such experiences reported a shift in how they conceptualize dying. So it turns out the paranormal may not make us afraid of the dead and death at all, but rather encourage the call to move forward.

The instinct to expand is something we all have deep within us. As I spoke of in lesson one, we have a natural urge to create and expand our awareness, and it comes in many different forms. The Universe is forever expanding and moving towards greater, and we have that same instinct built within us. Where things get mucky is when we begin to deny that expansion through our own negative thought and beliefs, but when we "croak," evidence points to a releasing of that resistance. If we can take a page from the Girl on the Butterfly Wing, Betsy, we must heed the message: "You are loved and cherished, dearly, forever. You have nothing to fear. There is nothing you can do wrong."

The eternalness of her message is repeated throughout spirit messages from all over the world, even when we insist on brushing it under the rug.

Other received quotes from channeled consciousness have included:

"You were born into a state of grace. It is impossible for you to leave it. You will die in a state of grace whether or not special

words are spoken for you, or water or oil is poured upon your head. You share this blessing with the animals and all other living things. You cannot fall out of grace, nor can it be taken from you. You can ignore it. You can hold beliefs that blind you to its existence. You will still be graced but unable to perceive your own uniqueness and integrity, and blind also to other attributes with which you are automatically gifted." – Seth, received by Jane Roberts

"Make fun of death. We are as dead as it gets, and we are fully aware of this joyous experience. We are with you every time you allow it. We are in every singing bird and in every joyful child. We are part of every delicious pulsing in your environment. We are not dead, and neither will you ever be. You will just get up one day, and get out of the movie." – Abraham, received by Esther Hicks

"Consciousness is personality touching the Universe at vital points." – S. T. C., received by Louis Benjamin

Isn't it interesting how the "dead" can call us home? How their awareness holds some of the deepest lessons? What I have found, after twenty years of paranormal research, is that they hold a far clearer picture of who we are than we do. If we could look in the mirror and see ourselves through their "eyes," we would be subject to a very different vision. If spirits teach us anything, it is to reimagine how we see ourselves, to take less of the physical into account and more of the nonphysical. They encourage us to care more about how we feel and spend as much time on our emotions as we do on our hair and nails, because when we understand that, the rest of our lives fall into line. They encourage us to find our joy now, not wait until we make our transition, and that we can have all of that while we are still physical here on this planet. And when we struggle in finding our alignment with our Source, our Core, again, they stand like a lighthouse calling us forward. They never waver and never join us in our pain, but they radiate a light that is ever steady and always beckoning. Perhaps Eben Alexander explained it best when he wrote:

"Even though I'd forgotten my life down here, I had remembered who I really and truly was out there. I was a citizen of a universe staggering in its vastness and complexity, and ruled entirely by love... Ultimately, none of us are orphans. We are all in the position I was, in that we have other family: beings who are watching and looking out for us – beings we have momentarily forgotten, but who, if we open ourselves to their presence, are waiting to help us navigate our time here on earth... Each and every one of us is deeply known and cared for by a Creator who cherishes us beyond any ability we have to comprehend."

LESSON 5
EVERYTHING YOU WANT IS ON THE OTHER
SIDE OF FEAR

"The opposite of love is not hate. It's fear." – Gary Zukav

~

T
HE MAGICAL LIFE OF EILEEN J. GARRETT
The paranormal is a magical place, and any good
author and reader knows that magical places are
filled with magical characters. Now, I don't mean magical in
the "princess and the dragon" sense, but parapsychology has a
way of demonstrating to us that magic exists in many forms
and presents a task to science that, at times, feels impossible,
yet it always manages to scamper along and catch up. Perhaps
that is one of the best things about parapsychology: it teaches
us that magic, monsters, and fantastic characters really do exist
in the brilliance of what we call reality.

Often, the simplest of characters are born from humble
beginnings sprinkled with a bit of mystery, and as we journey

with them, they become the greatest of heroes. The story of one such incredible and influential character (perhaps one of the most important in the book of scientific study and our journey into real magic) is that of Eileen Garrett: a young girl who would grow up to be one of the most revered mediums in the world and embark on a life adventure full of spiritualism, war, and romance, and ending in founding one of the world's leading centers in parapsychological study.

Eileen wasn't born into a famous family, nor was she a notable child in any way. In fact, she was so unremarkable there was even debate about her date of birth. Census records seem to show that she was born in County Meath, Ireland, on 14 March 1892, although most published accounts give the date as 7 March 1893. When she was seven months old, her mother tragically passed away, and she was sent to live with her aunt Martha and her uncle William on their family farm, and they decided to call her instead by her middle name, Jeannie.

Eileen spent most of her time alone, playing with the farm animals and connecting with nature. She had very few friends, and it wasn't long before she was considered a loner and the "weird kid," and that she should just be left by herself to play with her "imaginary friends."

Eileen had three imaginary companions, whom she later identified from photographs as deceased children from the neighborhood. By the time began school, she would say she felt no different than anyone else, but her peers felt differently, and she became increasingly aware that her perception of the world was vastly different than that of the other children.

Martha had no use for Eileen's imaginary friends or invisible playmates either. Any experience Eileen had was dismissed as a fantasy and the imagination of a silly little girl. The night that began to change everything for Eileen didn't arise until she was a little older. It was the first time she experienced the apparition of Martha's sister, Leone, and she noted that she was holding something. She looked outside and saw the woman struggling with a baby in her arms whom she didn't recognize. Immediately Eileen rushed to Leone's side to help her into the house. "I am going away now and must take the baby with me." Eileen fetched Martha, but when they looked for Leone, she had disappeared. Confused, Martha turned on Eileen, accusing her of lying and that she was being a naughty little girl. Eileen pleaded with her aunt that the apparition was indeed real and that she was telling the truth, but Martha would hear none of it. Eileen ran to her room, falling into her bed and bursting into tears. She cried herself to sleep, and when she awoke the next morning, she felt sick all over, angry with grief and depression and her body heavy with the weariness of a long night of tears.

She avoided her aunt for the rest of the afternoon, but that night at supper, Martha had news. She instructed Eileen that she was to leave the home and not return, for which Eileen was grateful. However, she was quickly sent to her room with no dinner at all, and later Martha informed her that the decision came on the heels of the news of Leone's death. She had died in childbirth the night Eileen had seen her, and Martha believed Eileen was solely responsible. Eileen was to be sent to a boarding school in Dublin, far from home, where she would learn how to act and behave as a "normal" girl.

Once studying in Dublin, Eileen kept to herself and her schoolwork, not divulging to anyone what she was experiencing in the supernatural. The boarding school was harsh and unforgiving and yet another place she didn't fit in. However, it didn't stop the experiences from occurring. The next spirit to pay her a visit was her uncle William, and his appearance was welcome. He had wonderful news to deliver: he told her that he understood her troubled relationship with Martha but nevertheless encouraged her to submit to her wishes whenever possible. William also said that in two years she would be free, as she would be going to London for study. Just as promised, within two years she was in South England, having been sent there due to a previous lung condition.

At age fifteen, Eileen's fortunes seemed to begin to take a turn for the better with her first real love, an architect named Clive Barry, who initially thought she was much older than she was. He took her on a whirlwind of romance, showing her the city and taking her to places she had never been before. She fell head over heels and slowly but surely began to trust him with her strange experiences and abilities. Clive welcomed them and, on that note, proposed to her. She accepted, and it seemed like her fairy tale was finally beginning to show signs of a happy ending. However, once they were married, something about Clive shifted and changed. He confronted her about her mediumship and told her she was to stop it immediately. He demanded she father his children, be a "proper hostess" to the friends he wanted to have over, and to keep her mouth shut about any feelings she may have had about it.

However, childbearing would prove almost impossible for her, and after the death of three of her babies, it was advised Eileen find some activities to occupy herself outside the home so she didn't fall into depression. She jumped into the role of helping others and creativity, working briefly for social services and then branching out into the world of comedy and theater. She loved the new energy it was bringing her; however, when Clive noticed her emotional shift from depression to joy, he immediately forbade it and locked her back in the family home.

Relegated once again into isolation, Eileen had no choice but to turn inwards. She became able to perceive the world through her fingertips, and "knowing" came to her more easily through the nape of her neck, her feet and her knees than through her eyes and ears. Clive began to notice that Eileen would have moments where she seemed to lose awareness and then begin talking about places and people no one else recognized. Concerned for her mental health, he sent her to a psychiatrist, but the consultation only convinced Eileen that she needed to come to terms with her experiences on her own.

Finally, after months of continued effort, Eileen became pregnant and had a healthy baby girl at age twenty-three, only to find out Clive had already gone elsewhere for a new wife. Their marriage collapsed, and Eileen fell in love soon after with another man. She predicted his passing due to a landmine explosion during the First World War and was confirmed correct.

Eileen fell into the arms of James Garrett, an old family friend who had ended up with a leg injury at a local hospital. As they visited, Eileen and James fell in love, and in 1918, she married him. For the next nine years, however, her abilities and the world of the paranormal began to consume her. Jim had no interest in it whatsoever, and no matter how Eileen tried to ignore her instinct and calling, she simply could not. Her love of the world she had glimpsed was so great and so powerful, her marriage ended after nine years, and she kept the last name of Garrett.

Determined to follow her dreams and a greater under-standing of what she knew to be true in her heart, Eileen found Edward Carpenter in 1919. In the two years she knew Carpen-ter, Garrett later wrote, she underwent the "most profound spiritual experience" of her life, "a sense of release, of being set free, of being reborn." Finally, she was on the path her inner guidance was calling her towards, and she knew beyond a shadow of a doubt, this was where she was meant to be. She wasn't crazy or having hallucinations, and she wasn't strange and outcast, she was a medium, and she had found her purpose. She had no idea this was only the beginning of her true adventure into what Carpenter called "cosmic conscious-ness," but she was ready for whatever was to come.

In 1926, Eileen met a man who claimed he was a clairvoy-ant, and like Carpenter, he would prove to be another vital contact. He told her he believed she had "latent powers" that encompassed a range of unique psychic abilities, includ-ing clairvoyance and clairaudience, distant healing, and psychometry. After accurately holding a watch he passed her and, using the process of psychometry, gaining accurate impressions from the watch, Eileen was introduced to the College of Psychic Studies, where she proved to have an influ-ence on table-tipping experiments. She also began to freely enter trances where she channeled a man named Uvani from the Orient. He would relay messages from deceased people to the sitting group.

As she moved about the world of spiritualism, Eileen wasn't entirely convinced her answers lay there. She began to branch outside of that circle and lean towards the scientific studies of Harry Price at the National Laboratory for Psychical Research. Throughout the 1930s, she volunteered her services wherever she could, seeking her own answers and helping any scientist who happened to be studying the psychic realm and survival after death. Eileen threw herself into the world of parapsychology, and the further down the rabbit hole she went, the more passionate she became. But trouble was brewing.

While in Germany, World War I was coming to an end... but World War II was fast on its heels. A growing darkness was descending over Europe in the form of swastikas and the red and black flag of the Nazi party. A sickness was beginning to spread, and knowing she was no longer safe to be speaking about psychic abilities in a growing communist regime, Eileen gathered her courage again and fled to France. Following her calling to help others, she immediately found a soup kitchen at an orphanage and began to pour her efforts towards helping the children in trouble, but soon the darkness spread. Germans flooded into France, the Nazis began to move their stronghold across the continent, destroying and pillaging cities and minds. Fearing for her life, Eileen got a flight to Portugal and barely escaped by the end of 1940.

In America, the war was an ever-popular subject, and the press was in full swing gathering whatever stories they could. Harrowing tales of air raids and hero soldiers flooded the news-papers. So when Eileen had contact with the spirit of a downed R-101 airship, which had crashed in France, the world's eyes turned to her. In Lisbon in 1940, Eileen was urged to go to America to continue lecturing, and she did so, taking to the lecture circuit with the support of the American Society for Psychical Research. However, she wasn't talking about mediumship or the science of psychometry – she was delivering psychic news reports of the goings-on in Europe as the Nazi terror reigned strong. Now residing in New York and with the assistance of her longtime friend Frances Payne Bolton, she established the Creative Age Press, and from there created the pinnacle of her endeavors: the Parapsychology Foundation, with the goal of supporting academic parapsychology. Soon her daughter, Eileen Coly, joined her in New York and took over the Parapsychology Foundation in her mother's honor.

Eileen never forgot her roots in nature, often returning to the French gardens to read once the war had come to an end. The call and connection that nature offered was forever intertwined with her knowledge of spirit and parapsychology – to her, they were inseparable. In September of 1970, while at the European residence of the Parapsychology Foundation and after holding the nineteenth international conference, Eileen was reading quietly in her garden when she suffered a heart attack. She was rushed to the hospital only to pass away in Nice at age seventy-eight. On that day, her questions were answered, and she became the very thing she loved so deeply: part of the nonphysical energy that she so loved and that called her home.

Today, the Parapsychology Foundation is run by her granddaughter and my friend, Lisette Coly, in the city of New York.

THE POWER OF FEAR

See, the emotional nature of fear doesn't stop us. What stops us is the unwillingness to be afraid and the unwillingness to encounter it. Humans have two major fears: rejection and the fear of fear. The nature of fear has never harmed anyone; what does the damage is our desperation to escape it. We want to be fearless, but fear is a façade of strength, and what allows us the courage to be afraid is the courage to stand up and do it anyways. *Everything you want is on the other side of fear.* There is no big dream or grand gesture that you'll find inside your comfort zone, and that's tough love and rough news for a lot of people. The question becomes "Are you willing to be afraid?"

Fear is not only one of the number one contenders that keeps us stuck in our ruts as we spoke of in the last lesson, it keeps us from the experiences we really want and often generates the experiences we are afraid of having. Dr. Phil McGraw has become famous for his phrase "You create what you fear," yet he couldn't be more correct. When we're vulnerable, we allow fear to circulate within us. We can breathe it in and release it like a tide, but if it is allowed to remain central within us, it blocks the river of well-being we have constantly accessible to us in the form of joy. Fear is a joy killer. Fear is a dream killer. There are people who will spend their entire lives putting off dreams because what they are telling themselves about the fear has them stuck.

Eileen Garrett struggled with fear, but the true warrior knows how to be afraid and not limit themselves at the same time. Your dream has to be bigger than the fear! We are never afraid of what we *think* we're afraid of. There is a saying that goes "Your greatest miracle is in your scary place," and every good leader is tested by fear. Your thoughts are either dragging you down or pulling you up. You can have the same everything: the same address, the same phone number, you can be in the same place as some of the greatest people in history or those you admire, and the thoughts won't change. It is the *level* in which you think that will change your world. Think about it: had Eileen Garrett thought on the level that Clive wanted her to think, her greatest accomplishments would never have been birthed. It is more comfortable for other people to have you in fear than it is for them to accommodate big thinking; it's just simply easier.

It always makes me smile when I hear investigators say that negative entities "feed on fear," when nothing could be further from the truth. They talk about it like these spirits are operating apart from the emotion, and the people having the experience and we know based on physics that this simply makes no sense. What we *experience* is a direct result of our thought and our thinking up until that moment when we encounter fear. These intelligences don't seem to feed on fear at all, but rather the momentum of the event builds with further focused thought. The more thoughts we think, the greater the momentum and frequency of our experiences, and if the essence of our thoughts is fear, the experiences delivered to us will match the *feeling* of what we think. We are rarely thinking about a frightening paranormal encounter when it happens to us, but I can promise you that you've got something going on within you that is resonating with the frequency of fear if you're experiencing fearful encounters. We get what we feel, not what we think about, and if you don't perceive your situation properly, you'll miss the solution. You've got to fly above something before you can see it with an eagle's-eye view. When we begin to make things mountains and negate our own role in their creation, we lose our destiny. If we make things mountains, we won't have the strength to climb them because usually when we make one thing a mountain, we have a tendency to do that often.

Rediscovering wonder means stepping out of rightness. One of the reasons Martha couldn't see Eileen's gifts was because her response to fear was to "fight for the rightness" of her own position. People have a tendency to become so attached to their own ideas they believe that if the idea or paradigm fails, that means *they* are a failure. Like I mentioned previously, mentors aren't always people. Failure is a mentor, and when we fear failure, we miss the lesson. If you don't want to fail, you don't want to be a part of the process, and it's that simple.

Following our instinct as Eileen did will inevitably bring you to failure and fear *at some point* in the journey. Not because you did anything wrong, but because it is a part of the process in the same way success is a stepping-stone as well. Parapsychology or anything else you dive into is not going to be a success-only journey, and in fact, science itself is not a success-only journey. There's the old adage of Thomas Edison speaking of creating a light bulb with over a thousand failed designs. His response to someone who asked why he hadn't succeeded yet was that he had simply found a thousand ways the light bulb won't work! Fear needs to be tended to if we are to follow our deepest callings. There is never a point in which it will disappear, but it needs to be managed or else it will present itself to you as a mountain you continuously add to until it is insur-mountable.

YOU CAN'T BE LOYAL TO FEAR

People are stressed to death by their imagination! What-ifs and maybes, beliefs and counter-beliefs, television shows and what other people are telling them. They are so engrossed with what the heart feels, they often haven't considered what the head thinks. In order to really understand instinct, there is a balance, because without thought, we can't act on our calling. Where head and heart balance equals clear instinct. You will never win a battle if you are feeling too much and ignoring what you know. Real decisions that move your life will come from your head and not only your feelings because feelings are fickle. How many times have you heard "I'm just not feeling it right now" or "I'm just not into it today, I don't feel like it"? I'll tell you one thing I've learned for certain, every time you do, you cancel out opportunity with the underlying fear. If you lose your head, you lose your government because our heads govern the steps we need to act on our instinct. Your emotions and fear will cause you to forfeit your opportunities. No one has time to babysit your feelings if you can't separate the emotion from the thought! You can't be loyal to fear and expect a new thing to manifest.

In a haunted home when people are afraid, it is almost always because they are driven by the *imagination* of what they feel might happen next. Their world is often consumed to the narrow vision of a straw because they are so hyper-focused and married to the fear that's being created. So often we are loyal to the wrong things! We chat up health and functioning, but we are loyal to the dysfunction because it's what we know. It's not always that fear is easier, but it can be more familiar, and the unknown of what's coming can be the thing we fear the most. People tend to fear the fear itself more than the uncomfortable feeling of the unknown, and even though it can lead to positive possibilities, many times our minds tend to drudge up all the terrifying ideas rather than the happy notions. This is where our internal stories either serve us or hinder us. What we tell ourselves during a period of fear will determine how we come out of that period in our lives.

There are times when fear truly is a decision. You can be afraid and choose not to stay there. When I was taking clients years ago, this was always a principle that stuck out as a game changer for them. When they realized they could approach the paranormal in a different way and the direction they chose was their own, it brought the power back to their experience. One of the best ways to tame fear is to realize that our emotions are often driven by our story. When we change the story and the framework, our imaginations begin to receive new thought. Here's the thing I really want you to get: we attract our thoughts. Many times, we have been taught that situations cause our emotions, and then we think about the situation that causes us more pain. But here's the reality: situations are neutral. We have the power to make situations good, bad or ugly, and the designation we give to them propels our emotions about them. Thoughts are the precursor to all things and matter. Thoughts themselves can be measured and exist on a few levels of reality. When we are feeling strong emotion, we are birthing thoughts, things, ideas, realities and probabilities that correspond with that emotion. We attract thought just as we attract experiences. Fear is no different, and on the other side of that uncomfortable place is often the healing or experience we are looking for.

That's the rub: everything you want is on the other side of fear. There is nothing in your comfort zone that will get you to the place you want to be because if it really did exist there, you'd already have it. And many times, our unwillingness to experience uncomfortable emotion keeps us stuck in the very thing we don't want. I have dealt with clients dealing with some of the most frightening paranormal activity imaginable, and they simply refuse to work through their own emotional junk to fix the reality they are receiving in their homes or businesses. The very idea of being uncomfortable with something they don't know yet causes them to hole up with the monsters in their house and in their head, even when it means physical harm to their family and themselves. Sounds crazy? Before you throw on the Judge Judy robes, think about your own life experience. What have you refused to move through to follow your heart and instinct because fear stepped in the way? We've all done it. Maybe it was an abusive relationship, a business you didn't chase, an idea you gave up on, or a person you didn't talk to. In the end, my clients all have one reality: the place they don't want to go is where their healing is.

This is where faith and instinct start to really play a role. Without the faith to pull through the experience of confronting fear, fear will rear its ugly head, and you'll go running. Eileen Garrett had many monsters to face, including the fear of the Nazi engine sweeping through the countries she so loved.

Although Hitler had a fascination and strong interest in the occult and psychic work, a freelance medium spreading the good tidings of the opposition would never have been tolerated. Being caught would have spelled certain execution. But for Eileen, fear likely visited her in many ways. There were long periods of her life where she learned to be alone and to love her own company, and also periods of time where those around her would have far rather seen her choke on their own narratives of who they wished she was rather than the person she was meant to be. Eileen's ability to write her own story probably saved her life. Sometimes we read tales like that and think our story is different, we didn't have to face down the Nazis, and maybe we weren't sent to harsh boarding schools. Our situations may differ, but fear comes in many colors, and how we tackle the challenges presented to us involve the same tasks and processes.

Part of what moved Eileen through these terrifying times was that her dream was simply bigger than the fear. We need to have goals larger than the fears we face so that when those come up, the instinct and calling overrides them. That's the problem with people who don't dream big enough and have convinced themselves of their own disappointment: when fear arises, and it will, there is nothing to chase beyond the fear. The fear becomes the end game, a wall at the end of a tunnel, and they lose the courage to move ahead. When you have no big dream for you, your business, your family or your life, you can get cut down at the knees by the first Martha who throws shade your way. The first Clive you run into who says, "This is ridiculous. You don't deserve to be who you are," will win that argument with one blow. Sure, you might fight back, but the fight won't last because the battle is in your head with those very seeds that have been planted and watered by the Clives who want to see you fall. In those times, you have to have such a clear vision in front of you that you refuse to carry on the battle in your mind once those people are out of your life.

Eileen's instinct was so clear, and her drive was so permeating that even a husband who was a generally good guy but didn't really support her in her mediumship was not in her plans. Because she was happy in her own company, letting go of the naysayers wasn't a fear that was on her radar either. She knew the Universe would fill those holes with people who would come to support her, people like Frances Payne Bolton. She wasn't looking around hoping others would accept her or trying to drag people like a ball and chain to the finish line of her own dreams; she knew that if she let them go, the right people would find her. So often we lose the sight and sound of our instinct and vision because we fear what other people might think or do about it. Had Eileen pandered to Martha's vision of who she wanted her to be, she would have never made it out of the gate to finally fulfill her purpose in the field of parapsychology.

Fear is a tool for many people. Doubt and fear can be wielded like a physical weapon and can deal a blow that can devastate your life if you don't have a good relationship with your own fear. The fear of losing others can stop someone cold if they don't have a vision that surpasses the manipulation. That weapon has a dull edge if you have already made peace with the idea that fear will be a part of the journey to a greater future. Life coach and spiritual teacher Iyanla Vanzant once said: "If you don't have pee running down your leg at the thought of your dream, you're not dreaming big enough!"

Whether it is your parents, your peers or societal expectations, some of the people you will meet will wield fear like a sword. In many cases of paranormal activity I have encountered, religion can be a tool for the same thing. Adults and even children who have mediumship abilities like Garrett will recount to me times in their own lives where the fear of religious persecution from the family or church was a prominent reason they never came forward with their experiences or abilities. It wasn't until later into adult life or working through their own emotional hurdles that they began to realize the fear of ridicule was holding them back from the freedom they longed for, and that freedom meant letting go of the fear they ultimately were hanging on to. It isn't until the dream for authenticity and freedom is large enough that they put down the story they've continued on behalf of their parents or teachers that they pursue their instinct towards the freedom they know they deserve. Fear is a great way for people to put a stop to a dream they find threatening.

In cases of inhuman or negative entities, fear can be used like a tool to keep order or maintain control in a home. In the end, those beings can be far less manipulative than actual human beings walking around on the planet! They have no fear of rejection or feelings of jealousy and don't often care about your own visions of success for the future. They are egocentric and very much about whatever is going on in the moment, not a year down the road, almost like an animal. They may use fear as a way to get what they want for that instant, but once the moment is over, they usually move on quite quickly. They bare their teeth, so to speak, and off they go onto the next experience. The great thing about negative entities like this is that they don't hang on to a story. They have no narrative to keep up, and although fear can be a tool in their arsenal, they don't ever seem to have a vision for their future or yours, for that matter. While people often carry grievances and upsets for decades, these entities are very single-minded, and I find them often far easier to deal with than a human narcissist or someone with sociopathic tendencies. They won't deal low blows and passive-aggression, nor will they tell you they will disown you if you pursue your passion! See, we don't care about threats and fear from those we don't know, or at least we don't care nearly as much. The hardest part of maintaining a vision as big and as wild as Eileen Garrett's or J. B. Rhine's is that the fear can be tossed into the mix from the outside.

Here's where the decision part really makes all the difference. A ship can't sink from the outside. Icebergs may hit, and storms might blast against the hull, but unless the water seeps in and the outside influences blow a big enough hole in the bow, that ship isn't going under. Part of what will keep your hull and bow together will be your vision. If you've given enough momentum to the faith of your vision and you know your instinct and inner being is giving you the right information, those attacks can come, and they may cause a few dents, but nothing that you and your crew can't easily repair. Interestingly, in homes struggling with frightening paranormal phenomenon, the closer the family is emotionally and the more support they receive from within is a huge indicator of their success rate. The crew is already working in tandem to reach a broader vision, so when the fear hits, the dents in the ship become a lot easier to weather. Part of what made Eileen Garrett so successful was her ability and instinct to find the people she needed to support her vision, and her wisdom to let those go who couldn't see it.

It was once said that slave owners were told the following: "You are allowed to teach the slaves to do anything... but read."

If you have it in your head, you can have it in your life, and once a dream has nested, it is a very hard thing to diminish and beat down again. For those wise enough to manage their fear, feel it, and do it anyways, a dream is a calling that cannot be doused. In the days of the slave trade, this was a widely known fact. Keep people in fear, and inner guidance becomes almost untenable. Although never an African-American slave, Eileen Garrett's severely abusive relationship had the potential of isolating her from her mediumship abilities as well as her own joy. Going with the flow Clive had dictated for her and the household would have been a less argumentative road, but Eileen discovered peace at any price was no peace. Make no mistake: people who have no dreams will try to kill yours.

That's the power of a calling and following instinct. When we buck the current, misery is the inevitable end. The joy and freedom we seek is on the other side of everything we don't want to confront, and the gift that the paranormal can bring us is not simply that we will have nicer spirits to live with (although that is a wonderful side effect), but that those who made a difference in the field of parapsychology and in under-standing humanity faced fear and did it anyways. Eileen Garrett had no idea whatsoever as she was being outcast by her friends at school or as she was spending her days connecting with animals at the farm that she would one day change the world with the very thing that made her so hated. The one gift she was told to bury, and fear was the very thing she had to embrace to find her place in the world.

Vision is the ultimate enemy of fear. When you have a vision, fear is humbled in its presence. It isn't that it will stay quiet; in fact, it is just the opposite. The bigger the vision, the more fear will rise to meet it. This is usually the point in the road where the majority of people turn around. Even in paranormal investigation, fear is usually the point at which most people run out the door, but the answers aren't where you came from, and we've got to get that as humans. The answers are never where we were because the Universe doesn't look backwards, the vision and the answers are always forward. Sometimes, the reason we run out the door is that we are simply not ready to accept the unknown that is coming, and sometimes it's because we start letting the child take the driver's seat rather than the adult. Because fear can be a learned response, we have to check in with ourselves and really examine which part of who we *are* or who we *were* is making the decisions. Sometimes fear of the unknown or the future comes from the fact we are still letting the child version of our beliefs or stories drive the vehicle of our vision, and as soon as that happens, fear kicks in.

Eileen Garrett's life sets a stunning example for all of us who come after her. There is a piece of all people to be found in each part of her life and a lesson to be garnered in each step and decision. If your life is stalled because of fear, the question for you to ask is this: How big is your vision? Parapsychology is all about expansion, possibilities, and reshaping your reality, something Eileen understood deeply through her own self-discovery. The journey is yours, no one can do it for you, but it is a sure thing that everything you have ever dreamed is on the other side of fear. And when you embrace and welcome that with open arms, when you make peace with the idea that fear does not come because you're doing something wrong, it becomes a welcome part of the process of success and joy. After a while, you begin to feel fear and say, "Yes! I'm dreaming big enough!" It becomes part of the adventure. Just because you feel fear doesn't mean your instincts are wrong; in fact, they are doing exactly what they should be doing! Your next decision is to move with it or move against it. One will take you where you need to be; the other will stall your life until you make a different choice. Remember, you need all the pieces on your journey, and one of those pieces will be fear. How you choose to move with it will change your outcomes, possibilities, potentials, and ultimately the course of your life.

Dr. Joseph Banks Rhine

Dr. Joseph Banks Rhine

Maurice Grosse

Maurice Grosse

Dr. Carl Jung

Napoleon Hill

Robert Monroe

Neville Goddard

Eileen Garrett

Dr. Eben Alexander

Dr. William Roll

Dr. Scott Rogo

LESSON 6
OUR PHYSICAL EXPERIENCE IS ABOUT
TRANSITION...USE IT

"A place belongs forever to whoever claims it hardest, remembers it most obsessively, wrenches it from itself, shapes it, renders it, loves it so radically that he remakes it in his own image."
— Joan Didion

~

HE TRAUMA OF TRANSITION
In the world of the paranormal, we hear the word "transition" a lot. I work on two shows, *Paranormal 911* and *Haunted Hospitals*, and the idea of transitioning because of the death process is a topic we discuss in every season. On the show, nurses, doctors, first responders and caregivers discuss how transition has become a part of their everyday world, and they get a glimpse of the paranormal in between. Sometimes it's because of an apparition, a patient reports a

near-death experience, or their own encounter with a hospital spirit. These amazing healthcare professionals are a solid reminder that our physical experience here is short and can end when we least expect it. Many people just assume they have time because they haven't reached eighty years old, or they assume because they are healthy and well that they have a long life ahead of them. I can tell you from losing both my best friend Stephanie at age twenty-seven and my father in his early sixties to cancer that there is no age that death discounts.

They also relate the word "transition" to the death process almost exclusively. The reality is birth and death are very similar. It is said we "cry when they are born and rejoice when they die," and both experiences often carry a similar energy. Birth says I am transportation to the next dimension, and death says so am I, but there are many transformations in between. We're in transition whenever we have outgrown our environment's parameters or when something happens to us that will cause us to reposition ourselves.

You can find restrictions in your environment and with other people. Regardless there is trauma in transition and sometimes it is indeed the trauma of the traveler to transition to the next dimension. That next dimension isn't always the nonphysical; sometimes that next dimension is the next level of your life.

Interestingly, the card of death in the tarot decks stands for transition and transformation. It says you can't feed in one realm and stay there; eventually you will have to move dimensions and move into a place that will accommodate the expanded version of you. Just like a baby is birthed from a womb as it outgrows its mother, as we expand, we must transition as well. We get to a point where we have to say "I've got too much going on to stay in this hole. Either I have to get out, or I will suffocate where I am." These moments of transition happen when they happen, and it's not always comfortable. They often come at times when you don't expect it: there is no committee meeting or planning session and no chance to arrange the particulars. Instead, these pivotal moments come just when you think you've really got your balance in order to set you up to become a student again for the new phase of your life. Just as death is a process to transition us from one state of being to the next, these transitional moments in our physical life experience are designed to pull us, sometimes kicking and screaming, to the next phase of our expansion. Our biggest mistake is we think we have time, so we resist the transitions or remain in pain or uncomfortable places longer than we should. We're not meant to stay and eat only one thing at the buffet of life for the rest of our days! Our bodies need more than fried chicken to grow and heal and come to new conclusions about what we really want.

In transition periods, pain can often be the catalyst that inspires our move forward. It doesn't have to be, but it's rare people don't wait for a painful situation to re-evaluate where they are and what they're doing with their life. We peer through the bars of depression, watching others move ahead, and wonder why it isn't us, as if we have nothing to do with our experience. You can be dead and still breathing! Sometimes, it's a catalytic moment of tragedy that lines us up for a life shift we never saw coming, and it can be in the darkest places where our instinctual calling for more becomes the loudest. The paranormal has a wonderful ability to call us from dark places because it is the embodiment of the greater part of who we really are and calls us back to our nonphysical connection. We don't need the death process to happen in order to rediscover who we were meant to be, and it's my hope that it doesn't take tragedy for you to find your way through transition moments, but if it does, be prepared to be broken open before you're pieced back together.

MAURICE GROSSE & THE ENFIELD HAUNTING

Transition places can make you realize you are meant for more: to understand more, to be more, to know more. However, you may not have the ability or the pedigree to step into the new arena you're being called to; it might be that you just stepped into something you don't understand. You might not know how to dress for it or even have a reference for it, but it's happening anyways. These moments say "I'm here, but I look like my history and where I came from. I'm still bruised from what I went through to get here, but here we go. I'm ready anyways."

Maurice Grosse passed away in 2006 and left us a lesson in transition and position that has left an indelible mark on parapsychology and in the hearts of many who knew his story. Born in Hackney, London, the son of Russian and Jewish immigrants spent his childhood excelling in science. He even went as far as to construct a crystal radio for himself at a young age and quickly fell in love with engineering and the arts. Grosse joined the Territorial Army and during World War II, serving in the Royal Artillery and in 1944; he married and soon after had three wonderful children. With his passion for the arts and creativity, Maurice was an inventor at heart and spent most of his days creating brand-new gadgets and mechanical systems, which were incredibly successful. They sold all over the world under his company's name Maurice Grosse Displays, Ltd. Quickly becoming a member of the Royal Institution and the Institute of Patentees and Inventors, he created complex vending machines, moving billboards, as well as the first automatic newspaper dispenser. Maurice's success was enduring, and his family continued to love and support his wild ideas and unique inventions. However, his world changed one day in 1976, and nothing would ever be the same for Maurice again. It was a tragedy that not only called him higher, but thrust him into a position of transition and discovery.

One day in 1976, the call every parent fears the most came to Maurice's attention: his young daughter, Janet, was dead. She was killed in a motorcycle accident, her head injuries too severe to survive, and the inventor's life was forever changed. In pain and grief, Maurice's life was spun upside down, and the successful engineer was forced to re-examine what he thought he knew. These periods in our lives have a funny way of also revealing broader things, purposes and ideas and inspiration we could not see before, and for Maurice, a strange series of events began to follow. In the following days, Maurice began to notice a string of bizarre "coincidences," and after a time, he was forced to wonder if they were coincidences at all. He began to wonder if his daughter was really "gone," and his notion of survival after death began to expand. All incidents were suggestive of the idea that Janet was reaching out to continue the relationship with her father, and her father wasn't about to let go of that opportunity.

In 1977, Maurice joined the Society of Psychical Research and shifted his attention from engineering to something much larger: the study of consciousness and the survival of our personalities after death. Little did he know that Janet's death and his new pursuit in understanding this expansion would position him to champion for another little girl named Janet whom he had not yet met.

Sometimes, transition calls us to change course. We don't always get to choose when it happens; in fact, we rarely get to have a say at all. Suffering comes when we don't shift our gears and move with the tides that are flowing. "What we resist, persists," and when we hold ourselves back from that flowing current, we will be more miserable than what we think we already are. It takes courage to change course and move in the direction our instinct and our experiences take us, especially if it is way outside our comfort zone, which it often is. Transition periods are not about how comfortable we are; in fact, they are the polar opposite. They are often filled with upset, uncertainty, fear, and all-out crazy business! Humans don't like to be pulled out of what they know, but in order to move into the next arena of your experience, whether that be making a full transition to nonphysical through the death process or simply getting into a better position in your physical life, you have to be willing to leave pieces of where you were behind you. You don't have to forget where you came from, but you have to be willing to not stay there.

After a very short time at the SPR, Maurice noticed a case in the *Daily Mirror* newspaper that surprised him: a young family claiming they were being attacked by an unseen presence and were desperate for help. In Enfield, a suburb North of London, the paper stated that an unusual collection of strange phenomena was being documented and that the family was appealing to the SPR for an investigation, and very soon after, Grosse was officially contacted. Maurice jumped at the opportunity and prepared to meet the forty-seven-year-old single mother, Peggy, and her four children, having no concept of what he would find apart from what had been reported. Doors opening and closing, furniture and other household objects were allegedly moving around on their own, along with a plethora of other strange occurrences were all listed as observed at this small row house.

Peggy was terrified for both herself and her four young children, who were being ostracized in the community and amongst their peers for being the weird kids with the haunted house. Although the article in the *Daily Mirror* had attracted help, it also brought severe criticism. The low-income family was being accused at large of using the story as a way to seek fame and attention and maybe even a fat pay cheque. Despite over a hundred affidavits from police officers, neighbors, family and friends, the public still saw Peggy and her family, specifically her oldest daughter Janet, as attention-seeking liars.

Peggy Hodgson and her family were also thrust into transition. She was considered by her close neighbors and friends to be a conscientious person who loved her kids and worked hard to support them and make ends meet. The people who knew her well indicated she was a kind woman who had come by hard times as a newly single mother in an expensive economy. Her children were completely unique in personality: while Margaret (thirteen) was serious and reserved, Janet (twelve) was extroverted and playful. John (eleven) was rarely home as he boarded at a school elsewhere, and despite having a severe speech defect, Billy (seven) was a typical little boy. However, in this small three-bedroom council-owned semi-detached house, divorcee Peggy and her four children, Margaret, Janet, John and Billy, were living a nightmare. Struggling financially and dealing with the betrayal of her husband and their father, Janet was secretly delving into the spiritual, and the Hodgsons' inadvertently attracted the attention of a very unwelcome guest.

On August 31, 1977, Janet and John heard shuffling in their bedroom. When Peggy entered, a strange knocking sound began, and within moments, a chest of drawers moved eighteen inches across the room without any physical contact. Calling on their neighbors, the couple came over to investigate and also found no apparent cause for the knocking, let alone the movement of a full chest of drawers, and so, terrified, the police were called. WPC Heeps and PC Hyams arrived at around 1 a.m. Heeps witnessed a chair move three to four feet across the living room floor, and the knocking was now following the officers and the two neighbors around the house as if it had a conscious idea as to its surroundings and what was in them. Heeps testified to the investigators as follows:

"On Thursday 1st September 1977 at approximately 1am, I was on duty in my capacity as a policewoman, when I received a radio message to 284, Wood [sic] St, Enfield. I went to this address where I found a number of people standing in the living room. I was told by the occupier of this house that strange things had been happening during the last few nights and that they believed that the house was haunted. Myself and another PC entered the living room of the house and the occupier switched off the lights. Almost immediately I heard the sound of knocking on the wall that backs onto the next door neighbour's house. There were four distinct taps on the wall and then silence. About two minutes later I heard more tapping, but this time it was coming from a different wall, again it was a distinctive peal of four taps. The PC and the neighbours checked the walls, attic and pipes, but could find nothing to explain the knockings.

"The PC and the neighbours all went into the kitchen to check the refrigerator pipes, etc., leaving the family and myself in the living room. The lights in the living room were switched off again and within a few minutes the eldest son pointed to a chair which was standing next to the sofa. I looked at the chair and noticed that it was wobbling slightly from side to side, I then saw the chair slide across the floor towards the kitchen wall. It moved approximately 3-4 feet and then came to rest.

"At no time did it appear to leave the floor. I checked the chair but could find nothing to explain how it had moved. The lights were switched back on. Nothing else happened that night although we have later reports of disturbances at this address."

In the days to come, the activity escalated: toys flew around the house of their own volition, objects were thrown, and furniture moved on its own. Police, clergymen and other officials were all called in to help, and all witnessed the anomalies, yet the phenomenon was undeterred by the presence of guests. On September 4, Peggy's neighbors called the *Daily Mirror*, hoping the story would land in the lap of assistance for their dear friends, and thankfully, it caught the attention of two reporters who came to document the events. Reporter Douglas Bence and photographer Graham Morris visited the house, and Morris was promptly hit in the head so hard with a flying Lego block that it left a large bruise, which lasted for days. After another visit by two more senior reporters, the paper reached out to the Society for Psychical Research, who inevitably contacted Maurice. Senior reporter George Fallows reported as such:

> *"Because of the emotional atmosphere at the house and in the neighbourhood, ranging from hysteria through terror to excitement and tension, it has been difficult to record satisfactory data. Nevertheless, I am satisfied the overall impression of our investigation is reasonably accurate. To the best of our ability, we have eliminated the possibility of TOTAL trickery, although we have been able to simulate most of the phenomena. In my opinion this faking could only be done by an expert."*

Transitional moments have an interesting way of connecting people who otherwise may never have met. There is a power in the paranormal and in the Energy That Creates Worlds that calls us to new places and makes us pack our bags for destinations we never knew were on our itinerary, both emotionally and physically. Transition and travel can happen between nonphysical and physical, it can happen through destinations, and it can happen through ideas and paradigms. Either way, transitions can cause you to rendezvous with people you never knew existed and sometimes nonphysical energies you never thought possible.

Maurice visited the Hodgson house on September 5, bringing some calm to the terrified household and giving them guidelines to write down any incidents that continued to happen. On September 8, Grosse was welcomed to the house by a large crash and, at that moment, decided to take on the case for himself. Excited he may be getting a glimpse into the afterlife, Maurice's excitement quickly turned to concern. The incidents at the Hodgsons' home increased, and he began to realize he may indeed be in over his head as just one man and one set of eyes. Marbles that flew through the air and landed on the floor without rolling as if they were weighted with lead, doors and drawers that opened of their own accord, doors swung open violently, and stationary objects jumped and rattled. Maurice knew help was needed to document everything he was witnessing and called on Guy Playfair from the SPR to assist. Author and investigator Playfair responded to Grosse's plea and arrived on September 12 along with Rosalind Morris from BBC Radio 4, *The World this Weekend*. It was then that this case became more than what any of the men had bargained for.

Physical aggression began, and the presence in the house turned violent. Janet was picked up and moved around the room, Margaret was attacked and held down by an unknown force, fires broke out and then extinguished, leaving no sign of anything burnt, excrement was found around the home in inappropriate places, apparitions appeared and disappeared, the iron gate in front of the fireplace was deliberately wrenched from the wall, and then, in the most terrifying display they documented, the investigators began hearing a disembodied voice around poor Janet. What began as a gruff barking and growling began to form words, and the more attention and conversation it was given, the voice took shape until it could not only form words, but entire sentences. Intelligent, witty and verbally abusive, the voice behind the daily paranormal phenomenon appeared, and it even called itself a name: Bill.

Inhuman entities have a behavior that is common among them that Steph and I labeled as "the Wolf" after the term "wolf in sheep's clothing." It typically is a strategically designed identity often created with bits and pieces of old facts from the family or the home itself. It is not real, but rather a bluff created to imitate the likeness of a living person, gaining the trust and confidence of the investigators. The easiest way to tell if a case involves something like this is to look at the behavior of the intelligence itself. Old men named Bill don't usually go around ripping iron gates from fireplaces, starting mysterious fires, throwing little girls or, for that matter, barking and growling at researchers and police. In this case, the entity claimed its name was Bill Wilkins (a man who had indeed previously lived in the home) and went on to say, out loud with no audio equipment needed, that it had died in a chair from a hemorrhage in the living room. The seemingly coherent story, however, would change rampantly, as it does with most cases of negative entities like this, and it went on to say it also had sixty-eight dogs that would bite the head off

researchers if they tried to make it go away, nonsensical rant-
ings that sounded similar to toddlers making up a threat to
ward off their parents. Worried that Janet may be faking the
voice, Maurice devised a plan to ensure she wasn't trying
anything sneaky: he taped her mouth with duct tape and
continued to interview the entity. The voice continued to be
heard regardless, as was the case on future occasions when
Janet's mouth was also filled with water. When the sessions
were over, she would spit the water back into the glass,
disproving any sort of trickery or ventriloquism.

Hours of voice recordings were made as the entity that
called itself Bill ranted, stole objects, cussed them out, and
humored their questions in between growls and animal-like
barks, all while aggressively attacking Janet in spontaneous
bursts of psychokinetic energy. As the family suffered, public
opinion was riled. Now that the press had caught on to the
case, the plea for help, which had been initiated in good faith,
had now become a circus, and Janet was suffering. Emotionally
beaten down and publicly humiliated as a fraud and a liar, her
isolation was ever looming. Unable to go to school any longer,
Janet was a recluse at home under the direction and orders of
the abusive personality "Bill."

Part of transition is coming under fire. Instinct has movement. Instinct has rhythm. When you are in a period of transition, you will come under fire. That could be from other people,
situations, circumstances, or it can be from your own story
about the situation. Regardless, the fire is designed to keep you
from going back to the place the Universe is trying to move you
from. Maurice was under fire, and in his case, he was under fire
from the media, a nonphysical entity that was far beyond his

pay grade, and his new role as Janet's champion. Sometimes opportunities and our purpose come in the guise of pain. It's hard to recognize well-being in a storm, but sometimes that's where it needs to come from in order for us to get to where we need to be. Maurice was seeking proof of life after death, and he found himself so far outside his comfort zone, standing for a little girl against quite a few monsters in various forms, and he would in no way have been in that position to respond to that call for help had his deceased daughter not inspired him to seek connection. In my twenty years of paranormal research and having had many relationships transitioned by the death experience, I have realized that sometimes the purpose or the "lesson" appears agreed upon before you get here to this physical planet.

Janet and Maurice were under fire. Media coverage sensationalized the events in newspapers, with headlines such as "Terror for family in spook riddle," "Ghost hunters clash over mystery of spook or spoof kids," and "Phantom Fred is a force to fear" (accompanied by a ghostly image of Playfair). In an attempt to debunk the situation entirely, Melvyn Harris, notorious for his skepticism, analyzed the photographs of Janet levitating in Guy's eventual book about the case, *This House is Haunted*, and claimed they were clearly hoaxed by girls who were just being pranksters and demonstrated no paranormal events at all. In reply, Playfair defended the photographs:

"On the curtain-twisting sequence, [Harris] suggests that the curtain 'has simply been hit by the bedclothes and knocked off the window-ledge.' He does not explain how the curtain then moves into the room, as it can plainly be seen to do in the first picture,

instead of towards the window, as one might expect. Nor does he explain how it moves to the right, the opposite direction to that of the bedclothes, and then twists into a tight spiral. In the pillow sequence, he does not explain how the top pillow doubles up in mid-air and changes direction, which it clearly does. Had both pillows been thrown (with one hand) by Rose, they would presumably have followed the same trajectory and landed together, which they do not. Such movements, he says, 'easily correspond with those to be found in commonplace, everyday events.' Not in the world I live in."

Despite the attacks, Maurice stood unwavering at young Janet's side like a father to his own daughter. At age forty-five, Janet recounted her fear at the time in an interview:

"I knew when the voices were happening, of course, it felt like something was behind me all of the time. They did all sorts of tests, filling my mouth with water and so on, but the voices still came out. The levitation was scary, because you didn't know where you were going to land. I remember a curtain being wound around my neck, I was screaming, I thought I was going to die."

Maurice's love and loyalty kept him at Janet's side throughout the abuse from "Bill," and once she left the home, the events seemed to dissipate, although her mother, Peggy, who remained there until her death, was adamant the entity was still residing in the home. Maurice spent the rest of his life defending young Janet. Committed and certain about their research, he stepped back into the role of Janet's champion, a role that had been previously cut short with the death of his young daughter. Grosse wrote articles, spoke at conferences and made numerous television appearances to stand center stage for the bullied and ostracized Janet Hodgson. In 1995, he took part in the popular TV show *Strange but True* with presenter Michael Aspel. Two years after that, a verbal assault came from psychologist Nicholas Humphries in Channel 4's *Is There Anybody There,* and he immediately appeared in its *Right to Reply* TV program to give his version of events and defend the SPR.

Nothing just happens. Everyone has been given something to give to the present. We didn't come here to be complacent, and often when we think it's over, it's not. Many times we are simply taking score too soon, and when we do, we get stuck in the transition period because we are so concerned with looking in our rearview mirrors. Don't close the book in the middle of the novel when you hit a bad chapter; how often is the conclusion of the book found halfway through reading? Nothing we go through is wasted! The Universe has a way of utilizing our experiences, even the negative ones, for something greater that we may or may not understand in the moment. This is the essence of instinct and faith, and this is where we draw on it the most. When we get repositioned, sometimes it's because we choose to, and other times we are repositioned because of circumstances. In those cases, it is imperative that we find our sea legs in both faith and instinct, whatever that looks like for you. There is no wrong or right way to do it; these things look different for everyone, no matter your background, culture, religion (if you have one), or your history. But a repositioning into the next level of who we are is always on the way, it is part of the journey no matter what we do, and connecting back with that instinct and that center will turn into the long vision that will get you through.

Transition periods often mean we're being called to something new, and it may not look like what we want it to look like. In fact, in many cases, we would probably design it in a completely different way if given the chance or require the Universe to give us a few months' warning! I'm sure Maurice would have loved a degree or two before being thrown into the midst of Enfield, time to gather a team, and weeks to research how to deal with an invisible opponent. In the same light, he probably would have hoped for advance notice of Janet's motorcycle accident and turned the tables in a different way. But transition periods aren't like that: they force us to think on our feet, to heal in new ways, and to tune in to the deepest part of our instinct to hear the call forward. In my experience, nonphysical beckons to us constantly in a stream of well-being and abundance that is ever accessible. Maurice summed up his research best in an unfinished memoir he was in the process of authoring before he died. In it he wrote:

> *"The evidence, as far as I am concerned, is weighted heavily in the direction of the mind being a spiritual entity that controls the mechanism of the brain. I believe it operates in a dimension that can only be theoretically perceived with our present knowledge, although the anomalies displayed in the study of quantum physics may one day help to explain this extraordinary relationship. It may be, of course, that while we retain our physical bodies within the confines of our five senses, it is impossible to understand the complexities of a nonphysical existence and the influence it may have on our everyday experiences.*

"Putting the case for psychic research has never been easy. Researchers have to overcome many obstacles when presenting the results of their labours to the wider community. There appears to be a strong undercurrent of belief that what is not understood does not exist. It may stem from a very deep-rooted fear of the unknown or just a refusal to recognise anything that cannot be appreciated by our senses. This type of refusal might at first glance appear to be a sensible and logical way to approach our particular subject because we are dealing with the inexplicable. Yet are not other branches of research also dealing with much that is unknown and inexplicable?"

Parapsychology is all about the in-between. It represents that part of life that hangs in the middle between need and opportunity, where the information we got in the first phase of our experience ends and a new phase begins. The unknown reigns supreme here, and we are left with a book of information that needs to be evaluated if we're to move on to the next level life is calling us towards. The level of information we receive brings us to a place, and when it stops, we often don't know what to do. Who am I without this job? Who am I without this label? Who am I without this peer group? Who am I without being a father? Maurice had years of defining himself as being a father and inventor, and now he was thrust into an arena where he was off balance. Transition places are tricky because we can either lose ourselves or redefine ourselves, and some-times we have to lose what we had in order to be birthed into what we are becoming. We know we don't want to reinvent ourselves to fall under someone else's label, we've been there and done that, but transition places call us to be something higher than ourselves. They call us to tap into authenticity. They call us to tap into our Core, as Dr. Eben Alexander titled it. Like Maurice, we start to question: what do I do now? And the answer to that lies in the bed of authentic connection with the greater part of who we are, the energetic self. The key is changing the question "why me?" to "what now?"

Getting a new dream is crucial to finding our way through the muck and mire transition can put us in. You need the strength to go forward in such a way that you can build again. It's about getting the energy to use what you learned in the first half of your life and use it for the second half, like a second wind. Imagine what would have happened if Maurice had gotten stuck on what he didn't have anymore. So many of us are receiving the instinct and call forward, the map through the transition place, and we get so focused on the rearview mirror that we miss the calling. There's a trap in talking about "the good ol' days" as if they are behind you and not in front of you, and if you're not careful, you'll miss those around you that are there to be the ambassadors to your next level of being.

There are people who will help you through the in-between places. Maurice found his at the Society of Psychical Research and in people like Guy Playfair. These are the people who also want expansion and are not willing to sit in what was; that's old news. They are raring to go, and they have the *instinct* to collaborate. A support system is crucial to navigating the in-between places, and we can't get introduced into the next arena without someone from the new place introducing us to where we're going. Previously, we talked about the Japanese concept of the moai. These are groups of life-long friends who are not only there for social, financial, and spiritual support, but they are committed to the expansion of who you are and are excited to journey with you.

Interestingly, this practice stems from Okinawa, Japan, which according to National Geographic, is one of the happiest places in the world. In fact, the Blue Zones, designated locations around the globe that are deemed to have the happiest people, all have a concept in place similar to this. These are not groups of people that do the same things as you, or eat the same food, or even have the same job. Often they are people who are quite different from you, and although they may occupy the same space, they may have very different spheres of influence. In my own circle, my closest friends consist of audio engineers, antique specialists, psychologists, professors, podcast hosts, lawyers, musicians, folklorists, cryptozoologists, social workers, and more. In the end, they all have a similar intention, and the support for expansion and well-being is the same. Whoever is being called to be your moai will get you out of the transition place. They will walk you through it and introduce you to the next phase of who you are becoming. In one of Maurice's 1977 recordings, he stated:

> *"Everybody's busy. They've all got excuses. But I'm also a very busy man, but I've found time to do it, and so have you [Playfair]. ... It's like all sorts of things in this life, Guy. I've lived a little bit longer than you, and I can tell you that it's always the same bloody story. Whenever you get involved in something like this, everybody's going bloody mad to get in on the act, but when it comes to doing the hard work, you've got to really get around and find them. They're very few and far between. I've done enough charity work in my time – I still do a lot of charity work – and it's*

always the same problem. You always get the bloody talkers and the doers." (MG2OBi, 36:58)

You have to make the decision to come out of the in-between with wings. You might be crawling in your transition place, hearing only the call of your inner self and instinct driving you forward. Maurice was knee-deep in the grief of losing his daughter; he was crawling. However, the instinct that we are more than what the situation tells us will call you ahead, even when the circumstances don't make it seem realistic. This is very important to understand: you'll get the instinct *before* you see it change in the physical.

Did you get that?

Let me repeat that: you'll get the instinct *before* you see it change in the physical.

Parapsychology and quantum physics will teach you: believe it, and *then* you'll see it. This is key to understanding this place of transition because otherwise, like Maurice, the circumstances may have the ability to swamp you. Your vision is your life preserver: "I may not have ___ but I've got the calling and the instinct to move towards it." The first manifestation out of the transition place is the instinct there is more, even if it is unexplainable and inexplicable. Remember:

"There appears to be a strong undercurrent of belief that what is not understood does not exist. It may stem from a very deep-rooted fear of the unknown or just a refusal to recognize anything that cannot be appreciated by our senses. This type of refusal might at first glance appear to be a sensible and logical way to

approach our particular subject because we are dealing with the inexplicable."

Need and intellect don't draw opportunity, but when you are able to follow instinct, the Universe will smell those opportunities out and respond if you're in the headspace to receive it. That's what it's there for, and it can serve as GPS to allow connection to your calling. It won't give you the answer, but it will be your Wi-Fi to the path you're looking for.

How will YOU come out of your transition space? Do you have a vision, or are you still looking backwards? Are you stuck in the might-have-beens, or are you ready to refocus and have the courage to move with the current? You may not get to choose the circumstances that the Universe will use to reposition you, and you may not even get to choose the timing, but you will be able to choose your navigational tools. You will get to choose what you're driving towards and whether or not you're even going forward. That decision and that outcome begins with you. You can't get it wrong, but you can get stuck. This is the opportunity for you to utilize this transition space as something that's *for you* rather than something that's against you. If you are about to transition, or maybe you're in the thick of it right now, I promise you, this is your moment. You get to design something new: What do you want next?

"Let us stop playing the skeptics' game. Let us stop falling into the trap of qualifying our positive results with an air of apology. It sends the wrong message to those who wish to listen. Let us admit openly and positively that there are such things as inexplicable phenomena. We do believe that our research is legitimate and of

great importance. Let us stop apologizing for the fact that we still cannot explain the phenomena, and may very well never reach that happy stage. We [the SPR] are not just a scientific society, but a society that leads a quest that is as important to humanity as any of the physical discoveries that dominate our lives today." *(Maurice Grosse, The Paranormal Review, Issue 24, October 2002, "After 120 Years Of Psychical Research – Confusion Abounds!" p. 9)*

LESSON 7
LEGENDS COULD BE TRUE, FALSE, BUT
THEY'RE ALWAYS RIGHT

I n a fascinating and fun conversation Mike Browne and I had on our podcast, *Supernatural Circumstances*, Folklore Professor Lynne McNeill of the University of Utah said something to us I will never forget: folklore and legends can be true, they can be false, but they are always right. After spending years looking at folklore and the thought forms that stem from it, this resonated with me in a way little else has. As we discussed this, she went on to explain that legends and folklore aren't about telling a make-believe story. Instead, it's more about explaining human experience, and often, elaborate stories followed these experiences.

The case we were discussing at the time was the Jersey Devil and where this strange pastiche of features could have come from. Did a woman named Deborah Leeds really have a devil's child that she cursed, and it still flies around the Pine Barrens of New Jersey today? What made the First Nations people of the area title it the Place of the Dragon before any such story was even invented? What creature was being seen before the story of the Leeds family began? The concept that folklore and legend often stem from experiences with the unknown and was not always individuals making up a story and then thinking it was real was a new concept for both of us. The question on the table became: what if the Jersey Devil is real and had absolutely nothing to do with the Leeds story at all? When I did some digging into the lore that the Devil was steeped in, I began to uncover some interesting ideas that applied to not only the haunted Pine Barrens, but to our understanding of the important role of lore in parapsychology and our lives.

THE DEVIL IS IN THE DETAILS

New Jersey, the state associated with urban sprawl and bustling highways, is not what many associate with its nickname, the Garden State. Primeval swamps and unfriendly soils lay deep in the woods of what is infamously known as the Pine Barrens: a seemingly endless stretch of trees, strange shadows, waterlogged marshes, tea-colored rivers, and a landscape that transports any visitor back in time to years where humans had not yet touched the continent. The very environment spawns images and dark dreams of devils... and *dragons*...

The Jersey Devil has become synonymous with legend. It has transfixed minds through books, pop culture, lore, and has even been recognized as the official state "demon." It is harder to find a stranger pastiche of creatures than this bizarre gargoyle-looking beast, but as witnesses have said: if you

THE GIFT OF INSTINCT

imagine a dragon, you're 75% of the way there. Its cloven hooves, long tail, spectacular leathery wings, horselike head, horns, and massive size have been stitched into the memories of all children who have heard the stories. The sound of hooves on the rooftops, the nearly silent flight of wings, and the graceful darkness it brings as its shadow swoops over cabins and trees brings nightmares to even the deepest sleepers.

But it *is* a nightmare. Or is it? As a paranormal researcher, the thing I've learned about legends is that there is often a kernel of truth somewhere in the middle. When you dig through the tales and lore, sometimes strange truths make an appearance if you keep your mind open. The factor that keeps them as lore is what the real world calls "insufficient evidence." Whether it be tracks, hair, DNA, or even a body, a lack of satisfying the one thing we can quantify, our physical senses, leaves beasts like the Jersey Devil under the dark cover of myth.

In *Man and Beast in American Comic Legend*, folklorist Richard Dorson outlines six-point criteria for establishing distinction among legendary creatures of American folklore. Dorson specifies that the qualifier must exist in oral tradition, inspire belief and conviction, become personalized and institutionalized, is fanciful or mythical, and contain a "comical side," which endears it to the American public. Accounts of the Jersey Devil predate printed works such as newspaper accounts, and belief in the creature persists today in culture and on shows such as *In Search of Monsters*. Skeptics believe the Jersey Devil to be nothing more than a creation of early English settlers, similar to bogeyman stories created and told by bored Pine Barren residents; the byproduct of the historical local disdain for the historic Leeds family; the misidentification of known animals; and rumors based on biased perceptions of the local rural population of the Pine Barren (known as Piney's). But just how deep does this strange legend really go? Have people really *seen* the Jersey Devil? For witnesses, the answer is a disturbing *yes*.

One such reported account was given to the television show *In Search of Monsters*. A man, fishing in the deep wilderness of the Pine Barrens, was watching a herd of deer relaxing and nibbling on the foliage. The day was still, calm. The odd bird barely made a noise in the whispers of the breeze. No other animals seemed near that day, but something was out of line with nature's force. A crack of branches, a sudden stirring. The deer were alert. Ears perked as another presence made itself known. A new smell on the wind as it tickled the deer's noses. Another snap of a stick, a black shape shifting, moving in the woods beside them – watching. Another predator was breathing in the dense woods. And then, an explosion. A burst of speed and blur and wings blew out of the trees like a firecracker. As the fisherman watched the deer run for their lives, trampling the earth to get away from the incoming assault, the man saw what he described as a large black creature with a horselike head. However, it was not lunging as a horse would gallop, with its shoulders and muscles undulating as it ran. Instead, it flew. It *glided* forward with lightning speed as if it were an arrow hunting its mark. Its feet never seemed to touch the ground as it pursued its prey with focus and fervor, the herd of herbivores running, hearts pounding, through the woods and disappearing with their predator into the deep dark of the Pine Barrens.

Many trace the history back as far as 1736, when a tale

began that gave the Jersey Devil another nickname still heard today: the Leeds Devil, birthed from a woman known now as Deborah Leeds or "Mother Leeds" in the old stories. Most of us know the legend well, a story retold in the film *Rosemary's Baby*: a woman gives birth to a cursed child, which becomes a demon or a devil. The tale of Mother Leeds tells of a woman who, upon birthing her thirteenth child, cursed him upon his birth with the words "Let this child be a devil," upon which it grew to its massive size almost immediately, sprouted wings, screamed, and took off into the Pine Barrens like a dragon unleashed. Historians, however, tell a different tale. Brian Regal, a historian of science at Kean University, contends that "colonial-era political intrigue" involving early New Jersey politicians Benjamin Franklin and Franklin's rival publisher Daniel Leeds (1651–1720) resulted in the Leeds family being described as "monsters," and it was Daniel Leeds' negative description as the "Leeds Devil" that created the later legend of the Jersey Devil.

Ostracized by his Quaker congregation after his 1687 publication of almanacs containing astrological symbols, cosmology, demonology, occultism and natural magic, Leeds' fellow Quakers deemed the astrology in these almanacs as too "pagan," and the almanacs were censored and destroyed by the local Quaker community. Not giving in to the demands of the local community's censorship, Leeds was labeled as a traitor for rejecting Quaker beliefs, and they subsequently dismissed Leeds as "evil."

Titan, Daniel's son, continued his father's legacy in his own writings, and their family crest began to be printed on the almanacs he was publishing. The crest depicted a wyvern: a dragon-headed beast with batlike wings and two clawed feet, eerily reminiscent of the depictions of the Jersey Devil. By the early 1800s, witnesses were beginning to come forward with accounts of a creature in the woods that they could not account for. The First Nations people of the area call the Pine Barrens "the place of the dragons" and lends those to wonder just what "dragon" they might be referring to, as they were settled there long before any feuding writers.

1909 marked the height of the Jersey Devil sightings, with newspaper reports doing their best to document the terrified people's frightening stories. Vigilante groups and hunters roamed the woods in search of the creature, some claiming to have fired upon it with no effect. Even the brother of Napoleon himself, Joseph, claimed to have fired a cannon at a winged beast he could not identify. The cannonball, he later stated, seemed to pass right through the creature, leaving it unharmed as it flew on. To this day, affidavits have been presented from police officers, hunters, hikers, and residents all claiming, throughout the years, to have been up close and personal with a bat-winged beast in the Pine Barrens of the Garden State, yet no photos exist, and no tracks have been cast.

Jeff Brunner of the Humane Society of New Jersey thinks the sandhill crane is the basis of the Jersey Devil stories, adding, "There are no photographs, no bones, no hard evidence whatsoever, and worst of all, no explanation of its origins that doesn't require belief in the supernatural."

However, perhaps both legend and belief are the point. While we tend to see nonphysical as a prerequisite for something being "fake," this flawed belief often creates a mental pitfall: if something is not physical, then it must not be real.

Scientifically, we know this is simply not true. Many things are not physical yet are still studied and accepted. Does insufficient evidence of the Jersey Devil make its existence obsolete? Perhaps, instead, we need to take a look at our definition of insufficiency itself. Is insufficiency the end of the story, or is it the beginning of the adventure? Is it the absence of joy, or is it the pinnacle for the beginning of new information? Is the joy in the legend itself, or are we rooted to the idea that we cannot take pleasure or curiosity in the idea until we have a body physically manifested in front of us? Regardless of the Jersey Devil's place in American history, cryptozoology, and our pop culture, this state demon continues to make its presence known in the Pine Barrens and across the world, sparking terror, imagination, and a pursuit of the grandest curiosity.

The Jersey Devil isn't alone, either. Monsters and whimsical beings grace the fields of cryptozoology and the paranormal in kind, yet often find their roots in strong cultural tradition and lore. Creatures like gugwe, chupacabra, the hodag, ghosts, sprites, and even the monstrous anti-Santa Krampus have found their way into pop culture and strike fear, mystery and wonder into the lives of adults and children alike. Almost always the stories serve a purpose. In the case of Krampus, it's quite easy to identify the purpose and origin of the monster: if you're a bad kid, you won't get a visit from Santa. Instead, you'll get an early visit from Krampus, who will kidnap you, beat you with his whipping stick, and you might never be heard from again! It's not hard to imagine frustrated parents forcing the image of this cruel critter on tantrum-making spoiled brats. But not all folklore is as easy to identify, and some began in a place we can simply no longer find. It's these creatures that cause us to ask: did the story begin first, or was the story crafted to explain the experience?

We have an instinct for storytelling, whether it is to explain our experiences or to carry on information and legacy. Folklore is the realism of the mind, and it is a connecting thread binding our humanity to our cultures: it is a glimpse into the human consciousness that *creates* our culture. Legends of monsters and whimsy don't always come from people simply "making up stories" for the sake of children's bedtime stories; they often allude to far greater truths if one is willing to listen in the right way. They are a peek into the mind and madness of humanity and make the darkest and strangest parts of our souls more acceptable. It's easier to talk about monsters in a fairy tale rather than at the office water cooler; lore simply makes them more manageable. It's always interesting to me how people dismiss these stories so readily yet still nail coffins shut or place amulets on doors to ward off bad luck or negative spirits. Many people still hang horseshoes or sleep with a nightlight despite their adamant belief that ghosts and monsters are but a fiction of the imagination. I can't even begin to list the number of people who have laughed at what I do as a paranormal researcher, but refuse to accompany me to a haunted place to stay the night. Labeling something as lore or a story is often a common way to make the unknown into a belief rather than a potential for new realities we might not yet understand completely.

Much of the lore we have come to know in the West stems from the First Nations people of the areas. The many tribes and bands are deeply rooted in unique and sacred stories and culture that is often dismissed as a superstition of the uneducated rather than examined as valuable information. This horrendous habit of dismissing the tales and warnings of the indigenous is not new, but it is something that needs to be re-evaluated. As we enter a new era where we begin to understand the power of thought and consciousness, the notion that fantastic things can be focused into reality is becoming a very real probability. We also must realize that each one of these stories and reports is key to understanding something about the environment and people from which it came. Whether you believe a monster like the Wendigo, an entity born of famine, isolation and murder in the winter months of the woods, is a living, breathing creature, a spirit, or simply a caricature of trauma, it is no less real in any of those forms. Its message is also no less potent and valid.

The Wendigo is a great example of one of those legends that goes back beyond our ability to find the beginning, which leaves open the question: what came first, the story or the Wendigo itself? The frightening thing is that we simply don't know. Are the tales of this cannibalistic monster possessing people and causing them to turn on their family an example of people trying to explain insanity driven by hunger and starvation? Or was this an entity, a water spirit, finally identified after it began wreaking havoc on isolated communities? Was the Jersey Devil really the product of a curse, or was the Leeds story a way for the Westerners to explain away the reason the indigenous people called the Pine Barrens "the Place of the Dragon"? Nightmares are brewed in the deepest recesses of the dark, and the darkest places are often within mankind's own inner sanctums. Nothing we do or think is separate from that which is around us, it is all connected, and how we tell our stories determines our reality. Everything is perception, and when we understand the perception of others, we can break down fear and understand ourselves as well.

Folklore is an internal journey even though the expression is very much external, and because of that, we can't negate the role of consciousness and thought when we discuss it. When a concept or consciousness is believed in to the point of having emotional impact, such as the Philip entity we discussed earlier, can something as monstrous as the Wendigo gain a consciousness? When we add thought to a thought form, it begins to shift and change and alter, which is exactly how folklore begins to change and develop. Folklorists have often noted that the way a story begins isn't always how the story turns out a century, or even decades, later. The descriptions of the creatures mould and shift as more cultures and tales are added to it; the Jersey Devil being a prime example. It's been described with a myriad of different features over the last hundred years: while some say they saw scales, others state it was covered in short fur. Some people described it with claws and taloned feet, while other people described hooves and kangaroo legs. The Wendigo has been seen as a bald, gray-like alien, as a canid-looking dogman monster, or a forest-type spirit with a huge set of towering antlers.

In parapsychology, varying descriptions of apparitions is relatively common. There have been many reports of multiple people all seeing an apparition of the same person, but each perceived it at a different age, for example. Some people have described seeing angel wings where others simply see beautiful orbs of bright light, depending on their background and beliefs. For some reason, this is far more accepted than multiple witnesses seeing a different version of a strange critter like the Jersey Devil, and perhaps that is simply because a line in drawn between physical and nonphysical, and for some reason these folklore creatures get dropped on the wrong side of the line. This doesn't negate the idea that a focused thought could possibly become an expression of psychokinetic energy and begin to respond as Philip did. Now, is there an entity that wanders the deep woods of Canada that is the very mirror of famine and cold, something that, if you are unlucky enough to see it, may cause possession and death? If the belief is there and people are no less dead, does it even matter? If consciousness can be birthed from focused thought, then maybe whether or not the Wendigo is a flesh and blood monster is a petty question compared to the overarching issue of belief and focus creating a psychokinetic expression of a fear. It could be that, within folklore itself, the legends may hide clues to big questions in parapsychology that might otherwise be dismissed as fairy tales.

The evidence trail for some of these folkloric monsters is where this begins to get complicated. Often these creatures seem to defy biology and the laws of common physics, such as the Jersey Devil living for a century or being shot with cannon fire only to shrug it off and keep going. The dogmen, giant upright canids that seem to roam country back roads and burial grounds, often demonstrate a very similar ability to defy injury and death. The Beast of Bray Road, first seen in 1936, still stalks Wisconsin's Bray Road to this day and is seen and heard as clearly today as it was in the thirties. Because of these long "life spans" and animal-like appearances, they can skip the definition of physical animal and end up in the realm of folklore.

The Jersey Devil is one of the few creatures in cryptid folklore that has a definitive backstory and perhaps lends us insight into how we perceive and deal with the unknown. The human condition likes to assign stories to things we can't explain, and within those stories are explanations on how unexplained things function in our lives. They also define a purpose, good or evil. It gives us a label to assign to unknown events and therefore gives us a blueprint of action against it, depending on the belief systems we hold. If we believe the Jersey Devil is a demon, as many priests or people of the cloth believe, then it can be "dealt with" through exorcism and ritual protection. If it is a physical animal undiscovered in the woods, then it is to be researched and discovered rather than banished through spiritualist means.

Assigning stories to things we don't understand is often how we deal with the unknown in our own lives as well. My journey with folklore started early, but the connection with parapsychology was not something I drew until later in my career when I realized that many of cases I was investigating were facts wrapped up with a lot of storytelling and beliefs on the part of the client. However, we can't always assume that these "stories" are a psychological coping mechanism either and that no event happened at all. Sometimes, they are humanity's best attempt with the little knowledge we have of the world to understand something that was not in our template of perceptual functioning. It doesn't mean the story is "make-believe." In fact, the majority of the time, folklore gets something right. In the case of the Jersey Devil, people are seeing a large, unknown creature that they cannot identify in the Pine Barrens, and it has been going on for over a hundred years.

Sometimes, the attempted explanations can be what actually does the damage. Where people usually get lost with the Devil story is that a woman, Mother Leeds, gave birth to a thirteenth child, cursed it, and it flew up the chimney never to be heard from again. I'm pretty sure most of us have thought, "That's a cute fairy tale," and moved on with our day. Often, the nature of the story can obscure and even dismiss the facts that we should be paying attention to. Hauntings often fall into this category as well, and I have had countless discussions with militant skeptics who insist there is no evidence for supernatural events because ghost hunting isn't real. Well, they are half right. Ghost hunting is filled with pitfalls, fallacies, incorrect techniques, make-believe evidence, assumptions and nearly zero science. Does that mean that parapsychology has no backing, evidence, or science involved? Absolutely not. In fact, the evidence for many of the ideas parapsychology pursues is overwhelming, and thousands of papers are published in academia every year supporting these theories. Unfortunately, this is also one of the few scientific fields where "evidence" is deliberately faked as well. Every time something is debunked, it gives fuel to those who refuse to look at the real facts, and they write everything off as "fake." It is an uphill battle for the scientists who are constantly combating false beliefs, ideas and media pushing an agenda that "ghost hunting" is real science and ignoring those who put legitimate studies on the table with fascinating and convincing results.

Folklore, however, gives us a glimpse into an important factor investigators fail to consider: the state of mind of the people perceiving the anomalous event. For example, the Jersey Devil sightings exploded during 1909 when war tensions were high and communities were under stress. The psychology of the people is always apparent in these stories, and their perception and reaction are just as important. People do not arm themselves and shut down schools for no reason. Whether you agree or disagree with their reason is another matter, but they don't do it for *no* reason. For me as a researcher, this is where things get interesting. When I was dealing with clients, the activity in their home or business was, at times, nearly irrelevant. It was their perception of what was happening and the story they were telling about it that proved the most impactful. Not only did it determine their state of expectation, but also determined whether or not they were stressed, depressed, excited, or indifferent about what was going on. In turn, this set up the dynamic of the household, staff, and what type of paranormal event may happen next. The energy you project is what you get back, and if they were in fear, you could almost guarantee they would be in line for yet another terrifying encounter. Usually, it wasn't because the event wasn't real, but rather the story they were telling about the event that caused the emotional response and perpetuated the activity itself. Their story did indeed get something right: something was going on in their home they couldn't explain. Was the story accurate? Maybe not. Did it matter? Not one bit if that's where their focus and attention was aimed.

WHAT CREATES A MONSTER?

It's difficult to make a single, definitive description about the folkloric vampire, though in Europe, there are some common elements: bloated, ruddy, purple – fat from the recent drinking of blood from victims. Not exactly the suave and sparkly image that we have today, is it? They sure weren't sweeping the ladies off their feet or yearning for undying love. Blood was often seen seeping from their mouth and nose, their left eye open, and it was usually clad in linen, not tuxedoes. Its dirty fingernails, teeth and hair were elongated, and usually fangs weren't a feature. While some folks described them as the "undead," many described them as living beings. In Slavic and Chinese traditions, if an animal of any kind jumped over a corpse, it had the potential of being one of the undead. A body with an untreated wound that had not been cared for with boiling water was also a potential hazard, and, in Russia, if you rebelled against the Orthodox Church, odds were you would probably be a vampire when you died. Why? Because you must have been a witch in life, of course!

The typical vampire we see depicted in films is not the only place we see elements of blood-drinking monsters. In crypto-zoology, a strange animal known as the chupacabra (or goat-sucker) is a constant and persistent risk to chickens, sheep, and other livestock. Animals are regularly found with puncture marks in their necks and the blood drained from the body, with no evidence of blood in the area. People have reported seeing a four-foot-tall creature with large eyes hanging around chicken coops, which they believe is the culprit, although descriptions vary wildly, and in the recent years, a strange hairless unidentified canine has donned the name. It is now photographed regularly and has been seen on police dash cams, as well as physical bodies recovered and stuffed.

No matter what lore or description you subscribe to, an age-old question appears from this muddle of legend: What creates a monster? Is it their frightening appearance? Their ability to come back from the dead? Their deadly attacks? Or does it have more to do with the innate fear of losing our own mental functions to something over which we have no control?

Many cases of similar creatures – the Leyak of Bali, the Asasabonam of Ghana, the Ekkimu of Mesopotamia, the Asema from Suriname and others – not only cause others to turn into otherworldly creatures, but in the case of the German Neuntoter (nine-tuter), it kills by spreading its own disease. Its name translates to "the Killer of Nine" because it is believed it takes nine days to die once you see the creature. In a similar fashion, the Wendigo or Witiko is feared for the same reason: if it attacks you, you not only risk death but risk becoming another Wendigo. Your family becomes your target, and the sense of "home" you once trusted becomes a battlefield. The Asema is known to seep through walls as bright balls of blue energy, draining the victim's blood while they sleep. Seeds, nails and garlic are the only hope of defending yourself against this energetic monster.

Many of the features we see in the vampire lore blanket the fear of losing our faculties and giving in to our most frightening primal ways: eating one another, and having no choice in the matter. It also highlights another fear: the fear of an attack we can't see coming. Whether it be a vampire that takes on the appearance of a ball of light, or a seductive lover, or a family member turned vicious: the attacks all come from places we don't expect and from people we trust, when we are at our most vulnerable and where we offer trust. The idea of feeling uncertain regarding what happens to us after we die also plays a role here. The vampire or the victims are stuck in some kind of "purgatory," a living hell they can't seem to escape without the relief of another person's actions, such as killing them in some specific way or ritual.

In the Bayou, the Rougarou falls to the same traditions: a werewolf curse that holds a person captive until someone cuts them and causes blood to spill. Only then, it is said, can they be cured. Although there are plenty of Rougarou tales and stories about how it came to be, the idea of a curse that someone cannot control is a theme through many. I see a similar stream of thinking in the world of hauntings, and as a researcher, I am often surprised at how many still adhere to the idea that spirits "get stuck" and need to be crossed over.

The fear of these vampire monsters has been so great over the years that people have become desperate to recognize these traits before they get hurt. Nowadays, we tend to reach out to psychology: seeking books on narcissism, psychopathy, or sociopathy to avoid potential human predators. We fear running into monsters that we simply don't see coming; being frightened our instinct might fail us and we might miss a critical warning sign. We translate this same behavior into our mythos as well: how do we stop the thing we can't see from sneaking up on us when we are unawares? One method of finding a vampire's grave involved leading a virgin boy through a graveyard or church grounds on a virgin stallion – the horse would supposedly balk at the grave in question. Generally a black horse was required, though in Albania it should be white. Holes appearing in the earth over a grave were taken as a sign of vampirism. Corpses thought to be vampires were generally described as having a healthier appearance than expected, plump and showing little or no signs of decomposition. Even poltergeists or psychokinetic activity has been blamed for the possibility of a vampire lurking about. Things, again, that we now know are often generated by the human themselves. So perhaps that is a clue.

The fear of other humans has been a long-held issue amongst the human race. We fear other cultures, other races, other belief systems, strangers, neighbors and especially dead bodies. The fear of dead bodies is come by honestly: we learned early on that bodies emit diseases and deadly gasses upon decomposition. They bring rats and bugs and plagues. We feared corpses for good reason, and couple that with a general fear of other humans hurting us in some way, it isn't hard to see how the psychology of the vampire begins to come together.

During the eighteenth century, there was a frenzy of vampire sightings in Eastern Europe, with frequent stakings and grave diggings to identify and kill the potential revenants. Even government officials engaged in the hunting and staking of vampires. Despite being called the Age of Enlightenment during which most folkloric legends were quelled, the belief in vampires increased dramatically. This resulted in mass hysteria throughout most of Europe. This controversy spread like wildfire and began when there was an outbreak of alleged vampire attacks in East Prussia in 1721 and in the Habsburg Monarchy from 1725 to 1734, which spread to other localities.

Two infamous vampire cases, the first to be officially

recorded, involved corpses from Serbia. One man was reported to have died at the age of sixty-two, but allegedly returned after his death, asking his son for food. When the son refused, he was found dead the following day. He supposedly returned and attacked some neighbors who died from loss of blood. In a second incident, an ex-soldier-turned-farmer, who allegedly was attacked by a vampire years before, died while haying. After his death, people began to die in the surrounding area, and it was widely believed that he had returned to prey on the neighbors. The two incidents were well-documented. Government officials examined the bodies, wrote case reports, and published books throughout Europe. The hysteria, commonly referred to as the "18th-Century Vampire Controversy," raged for a generation. The problem was exacerbated by rural epidemics of so-called vampire attacks, undoubtedly caused by the higher amount of superstition that was present in village communities, with locals digging up bodies and, in some cases, staking them.

Dom Augustine Calmet, a French theologian and scholar, published a comprehensive treatise in 1751 titled *Treatise on the Apparitions of Spirits and on Vampires or Revenants*, which investigated the existence of vampires, demons, and specters. Calmet conducted extensive research and amassed judicial reports of vampiric incidents and extensively researched theological and mythological accounts as well, using the scientific method in his analysis to come up with methods for determining the validity of cases of this nature. The controversy in Austria only ceased when Empress Maria Theresa of Austria sent her personal physician to investigate the claims of vampiric entities. He concluded that vampires did not exist, and the empress passed laws prohibiting the opening of graves and desecration of bodies, sounding the end of the vampire epidemics. Other European countries followed suit. Despite this condemnation, the vampire lived on in artistic works and in local folklore.

Although these creatures are still present in theatrical works, movies, and books today, the vampire begs bigger questions than simply an option for a Halloween costume. They are an opportunity to glimpse the deepest fears of humanity. For wherever vampire fears lurk exists a people who tread on unstable ground. The fear of the unknown and the willingness to believe that which we do not understand will ultimately kill us or destroy us in some way, gives way to beliefs that can do far more damage than a fanged monster sneaking into our rooms at night. It is the same fuel that causes accusations, isolation, a lack of critical thinking and invested understanding, and the closing of minds. Perhaps the greatest damage a vampire can do is not to show up at all, but rather the fear of the vampire itself is enough to begin to create a disease in the mind. If we fear thy neighbor, the plague of the vampire begins to seal doors, close windows, and shut down hearts. Strangers become threats and potential monsters with no evidentiary basis other than the rumor mill. Conversation stops, and a new plague begins without a vampire ever setting foot on the ground. This is where *how* we tell a story really becomes crucially important and why folklore itself, as well as the concept of passing down stories and knowledge, can either help or hinder us as a human race.

THE BRIEF TALE OF THE VAN METER VISITOR

Monsters and ghosts litter our history, dotting *I*'s and crossing the *T*'s of legends, lore, and the supernatural. In Western legend, especially in the wilds of small American towns, often the supernatural is clear, but the circumstances are not. Sometimes, the circumstances are more bizarre than the science or the answers can tell us, and the mystery remains nearly 120 years later.

In a tiny Iowa town known as Van Meter, the year 1903 brought a stranger to the streets and skies of the quiet homes and businesses. Sometimes it takes a lifetime to change a town, but in Van Meter, it took this otherworldly visitor less than a week to change lives and strike terror into the lives of the residents. Here, in this quaint place, you can unearth the tale of a legend before it dies with the old-timers of Van Meter, Iowa: the tale of the Van Meter Visitor.

In the fall of 1903, a coal mine was being dug. As the company eagerly dug deeper and deeper into the earth, locals began to wonder if they unleashed something far beyond what any of the men had bargained for. What could only be described now as a humanoid pterodactyl, a huge featherless, leathery-winged monster with a long beak or face, was seen sitting on the rooftops in the downtown main street. Half human, half animal, with a unique and startling feature: a bright shining light gleamed like an LED spotlight from its forehead, a light no one in 1903 had ever seen the likes of before. It glared into windows, blinding shopkeepers and residents as it hunted and searched for some unknown target. It came with a horrific stench and moved at speeds never seen or recorded in any known animal at the time. Shots were fired each time, first by implement dealer U. G. Griffith as it flew across building tops. The town doctor and bank cashier, Peter Dunn, separately saw the creature and opened fire. At no point did the creature flinch or falter at the gunshots, creating even more terror in the residents of Van Meter. Dunn even took a plaster cast of the "great three-toed tracks." The hardware store owner, O. V. White, was awakened from a dead sleep a night later to see the creature perched atop a telephone pole. He took aim and fired with no effect. This awakened Sidney Gregg, who had been sleeping in his store nearby. Gregg said the monster hopped like a kangaroo. A high school teacher reported the same type of odd movement from the monster.

Terrified the town was indeed under siege by a winged demon, the townsfolk did what they knew how to do: they rallied, pitchforks and torches in hand, and conspired to march on the now abandoned coal mine. Believing this was the origin of the monster's appearance because of an odd noise J. L. Platt Jr had heard coming from the bowels of the mine, they vowed to close its doors forever with one blast of dynamite. "Presently the noise opened up again, as though Satan and a regiment of imps were coming forth for battle," according to an article in the Des Moines *Daily News* on October 3, 1903. Two creatures presented themselves, standing to meet the charge. When they saw the armed threat, they sailed away in a brilliant light, only to return the next morning to rally an attack. "The reception they received would have sunk the Spanish fleet, but aside from unearthly noise and peculiar odor, they did not seem to mind it, but slowly descended the shaft of the old mine."

They disappeared into the deep dark of the mines.

Theories danced around that these creatures were some

sort of pterosaur, the likes of which have been reported across the United States in other areas such as North Carolina and Illinois. Matt Cartmill, professor emeritus of evolutionary anthropology at Duke University, said that it was highly unlikely people were seeing giant flying dinosaurs, but not impossible. "I can't believe that if there were living pterosaurs in North America, three centuries of naturalists, explorers, farmers, hunters, trappers and biologists would never have run across a single specimen, living or dead," Cartmill told Raleigh's *News and Observer*. "I'd rank it as being slightly more probable than living unicorns in Raleigh and Durham. But only slightly."

Does this explain the monster that crawled up from the mines in a small Iowa town over a hundred years ago? Was the creature the residents of Van Meter saw some sort of pterodactyl adapted to the dark of the underground? Or was it something entirely unknown? A glimpse of our deep earth that is still so vastly unexplored? Or, like Mothman, was it something else entirely: a monster from a universe yet unknown, or a drop-in from another galaxy altogether? Or is this a simple case of a frightening campfire story passed down over the last century to draw more people to the tiny town of Van Meter? Is this simply a tall tale, or is there more to this tale than meets the eye? Just like in the case of the Jersey Devil, people don't shut down an entire town for no reason. *Something* happened.

Folklore stories always have to be examined and questioned with knowledge, instinct and open-mindedness. It is easy to dismiss extravagant tales as fairy lore or fantastic thinking, but as we can see throughout the annals of history, much of the folklore has roots in real-world issues that can't be thrown aside. It doesn't mean we have to start believing in vampires, but to toss aside the notion that vampires or winged monsters are simply a fictional creation of Hollywood movies is a poor excuse. We also must, under any and all circumstances, examine the tales we are telling as truths and examine whether or not they are evidence driven or whether we are simply creating fact from fiction in our own personal lives and belief systems.

I am a firm believer that we know the truth when we hear it. Somewhere in the deep recesses of our instincts we know when someone tells us the truth. It may not be what we want to hear, and we might make up a pile of excuses to dismiss them, but I firmly believe that we know when someone gives us a dose of good medicine. We may kick and scream and argue, but somewhere we are usually smart enough to know when there's something not quite right about our thinking. By the same token, we also have the instinct to know (usually) when some piece of information simply doesn't sit right or when we aren't being told the truth. Sometimes a lie isn't just a lie, and very rarely is it so black and white. Tales and stories are very much the same, even though folklore is by no means a lie; they usually don't come "out of the blue" but rather have a core of substance that is worth examining. These stories give clues to cultural functioning, belief systems and even the social and psychological roots of some paranormal phenomena.

Another label that gets tossed around in relationship to tales such as the Wendigo and other folklore monsters is the idea that it can all be explained away through a label of mental illness, in the same way mediumship and experiences with after-death communication are often sorted. Hallucinations or poor or deficient neurological functioning is blamed for these anomalous experiences, yet there is strong evidence to suggest this is not the case at all, but rather an experience of perceptual awareness that is still being researched and documented. We must keep in mind the exploration of consciousness and what it even means for us a humans is in the early stages; we are by no means coming close to truly grasping in any quantifiable nature the power of not only who we are as individuals, but as a group consciousness. When we are exploring tales of magic and monsters, we have to keep in mind that even today, we tell ourselves tales of how things have happened in conflict, we retell deeds in our own favor, we embellish, and we pass on stories and jokes. This is not a phenomenon of old; this is something we still do today in the forms of social media, memes, and literature. One day, future generations will look back on our own perceptions of the world, paranormal and otherwise, and examine your own tales in the trail you have left behind. We can only hope that they read our stories with the same grace and care that we have read those left to us.

LESSON 8

EVERYTHING COMES THROUGH YOU, NOT TO YOU

This is probably one of the biggest life lessons the paranormal has to teach us, and I promise you, if you figure this one out for *yourself*, it will change your life. I'm not kidding, and I'm not making exaggerations. This is a big one, because it's the universal law most people get wrong, and it's the principles behind everything you are creating in your life experience. Yeah, it's that big.

Things don't come *to* you; they come *through* you.

There is a fundamental misunderstanding about the laws of the universe, and it's the idea that things are just randomly floating around outside of ourselves and we are at the mercy of whatever circumstances drop it in our lap. We think we've got nothing to do with it, everything just happens, and we are victims of other people, other places, and of our parents. I'm here to tell you: Stuff doesn't come *to* you. That puts it in the hands of someone else. It comes *through* you. Everything you have, everything you want, everything you dream of, already exists in a myriad of probabilities. Now, whether or not you'll access those probabilities and line up to the frequency of what you really want so you can receive it is another thing. However, it doesn't change the fact that everything we have, want, and are able to be is already available to us. So why don't we all have everything we want?

Let me tell you, the Universe is unlimited. It is absolutely, unequivocally unlimited. We can't get our little egos around the multitude of probabilities available to us that will get us what we want in life. We're not built for that type of conceptualization. However, there is one big factor that usually stops us from going after our potential and what we really want: stress. We start to feel stress, and we take that as a "sign from the Universe" that it wasn't meant to be, or we find ourselves uncomfortable and think it must be because we can't hack it. Let me give you a clue into the realm of human emotion, stress included: sometimes we need the stressors to put us under enough pressure to get our chemistry to change it into diamonds.

We take for granted how powerful our minds are, and nowhere highlights this better than parapsychology. If you were anything like me, you were taught growing up that our brain is finite. It's the sum of whatever information we put into it and nothing else; it has a limited potential and can only do what we teach it to do. We were also taught our brain and all that information resides inside our skull, and it cannot leave those synapses and chemicals. It is a stationary organ that only functions the way the books told us it functions, and once the brain is dead, that is it for us.

We've come a long way since those days, thankfully, but

most of us still have a cap on what we believe the brain is capable of doing or manifesting, and because of that, we often neglect its use. There is, perhaps, no better demonstration of your own power than in the realm and study of a phenomenon called psychokinesis. PK research covers a wide range of apparent psi phenomena, including poltergeist activity and the movement of objects, to influencing biological systems, from enzymes to human physiology, and perturbations on nonliving systems such as the behavior of tumbling dice and random number generators. Now, that all sounds real technical, but let me give you the Coles Notes version: it is the ability of your focused thoughts to change the outcomes, probabilities, and experiences of all that is around you. We're not just talking about bending spoons; we're talking about focusing what you want from a probable outcome into physical reality. I told you at the beginning this lesson had the potential to change your life, and I'm not kidding.

Now, what's interesting about PK is that it factors in something those other paranormal events, such as seeing apparitions or remote viewing or even channeling, doesn't: stress. While most other paranormal occurrences are documented when minds are wandering or in meditation, PK is not only documented during times of celebration and joy, but also during times of frustration and psychological pressure. In short, it takes a range of emotional states in order to get any results at all. In fact, without stressors, PK may have gone somewhat unnoticed because the majority of psychokinetic events in haunting scenarios are fuelled by some kind of psychological stress such as a poor family dynamic, a recurring upsetting event, or a job. The bottom line is psychokinesis happens under pressure.

Stress can make you move worlds, and you have a mind that can move objects without touching them. What are you doing with it?

∼

THE FASCINATING LIFE & STUDIES OF WILLIAM ROLL

In the 1970s through a survey of 116 poltergeist cases reported between 1612 and 1974, Dr. William Roll, a well-known parapsychologist, made a fascinating discovery: he found that the phenomena in 92 cases (79%) seemed to be associated with a particular individual, or two individuals in certain instances. Similarly, in a 1989 survey of 54 German poltergeist cases, Monika Huesmann and Friederike Schriever found that 63% were linked to a living person. Realizing what he had discovered, he and fellow parapsychologist J. Gaither Pratt proposed that much of this phenomenon wasn't disembodied spirits at all, but rather created by a living "agent" (a living person).

In 1958 they coined the term "recurrent spontaneous psychokinesis" (RSPK) as an alternate means of conceptualizing poltergeist phenomena.

William George Roll Jr. was born July 3, 1926, in Bremen, Germany, to his father, a vice-consul to Germany, and his Danish mother. They divorced when he was three, and already his journey was becoming a rocky one. William went with his mother to Copenhagen, and his father went off to war, where eventually, tragedy hit a second time. His mother sadly passed away very suddenly, and William's life was turned upside down yet again as he was passed to the care of a guardian. Anyone who has lost a parent, especially at a young age, can understand the level of stress someone so young had to endure at the passing of his mother while already feeling emotionally homeless because of the divorce and separation of his parents early on. Anyone who hasn't experienced that loss can surely empathize with a child going through such extreme pressure. It was during this time in his life, however, when the pressure began to pull something from young William that he felt he would not otherwise have experienced. He began having out-of-body experiences where he felt his consciousness leaving his body entirely and floating elsewhere in the room. He ended up confiding in his neighbor who had a keen interest in parapsychology and loaned him books on the subject, which he soon found he couldn't put down.

Stress will bring things out of you that you didn't know you had in you! Without the pressure, finding those pressurized diamonds would be impossible. Sometimes it takes stress to form the experiences you need to find the gifts you have or, in both the case of William Roll and Maurice Grosse, discover the next steps to something bigger than you've got on your current map.

William was used to a life of high stress, so it wasn't a leap when, in 1944, Roll joined the Danish resistance and worked as a courier for nine months before the country's liberation the following year. It was then he was successfully reunited with his father, who had come to work with General Eisenhower in attempts to restore the US embassies in Scandinavia. When he returned to America, he enrolled at the University of Berkeley in California and began his studies in psychology, sociology, and philosophy, but his heart had long ago found parapsychology, and he persuaded H. H. Price, a professor of Logic at Oxford, to take him on as a student. William knew he had found his calling and began work immediately, running the Oxford University Society for Psychical Research, which brought him into connection with leading British psi researchers. As we have seen and spoken about in other chapters, when you lead with your instinct, you'll attract those who know it, and that is exactly what happened with William. He soon transferred to Duke University under the watchful eye of J. B. Rhine until Rhine's retirement in 1964.

While working with J. B. Rhine, he investigated a plethora of poltergeist cases, including the famous Seaford Poltergeist, which was later turned into the Tobe Hooper film *Poltergeist*. Along with Pratt, Roll made a visit to the house of James and Lucille Herrmann in Seaford, Long Island, in New York State, unsure of what to expect. The couple believed that they were in conflict with their son, twelve-year-old Jimmy, whom they initially believed was throwing objects and being a general terror around the house, as Jimmy's proclamations of objects moving on their own only happened when Jimmy himself was in the room. That opinion had changed, however, when police officers called to the scene felt that the objects were being thrown too far for it to have been their son, and the couple began leaving out bottles of holy water to dispel what they felt was an "evil spirit." These would spill in an unexplained manner with sounds that mimicked an explosion. Roll and Pratt tried to imitate and recreate the explosions with bottles and dry ice, but when one exploded when no one was in the room, they began to realize it wasn't being hoaxed. By the end of an extensive investigation, they concluded that the disturbances were indeed being caused by Jimmy, but not in the way the parents initially thought. The investigators concluded that this was a case of psychokinesis, and Jimmy was inadvertently creating the phenomena from the inside out.

This was the beginning of a lifelong journey into the RSPK phenomenon, and being a scientist, William wanted to know *how* it worked, not just observe things that looked interesting. Others began joining in as well: parapsychologist Hal Puthoff had theorized that gravity and inertia may not affect an object if an RSPK agent (the person creating the activity itself) can affect zero-point energy (a sea of random electromagnetic fluctuations throughout space). Realizing that spatial distance was a factor in this phenomenon, William, along with co-authors D Burdick and WT Joines, analyzed this decline and determined that its properties did indeed make sense with the zero-point energy theory. William began to theorize that psychokinetic waves, emanating from the individual and motivated by emotions related to the objects, were first connecting to emotional energy-imprints on objects, then reduced their weight through zero-point energy and finally moved them. Sounds too sciencey? In short, emotionally charged thoughts become things and can influence our physical reality. What you feel is not just in your head or just in your imagination; you change your environment through your perception and your emotion – good or bad.

Life comes *through* you, not *to* you.

William conducted surveys and found that of 92 poltergeist cases where a likely agent, or person creating the manifestations, was identified, in 41% of cases the phenomena coincided with changes or family problems. Disruptive manifestations were easier to spot. Things like objects being thrown and other bothersome incidents seemed to mimic the energy of the emotions generating them, and they stuck out like a sore thumb. William began to realize just how important psychological testing had to be in parapsychology research and that people were intrinsically intertwined with what they are experiencing, not just within the paranormal activity but in life experiences in general. The universe is a mirror and reflects back to us the emotions we predominantly reside in. William went on to note:

> *"The red thread running through most of the cases I have investigated, or am familiar with, is tension in family situations or extensions of them... In general, we find hostility in the agent which cannot be expressed in normal ways, the main target for the anger being people with whom he [or she] is associated on a daily basis."*

Parapsychologist Scott Rogo agreed with this theory and then took it one step further, realizing that this wasn't the issue of an individual but of a dynamic in the house or business itself:

> *"... feelings of hostility, frustration, etc. were common among the entire family. Unfortunately, there was no real method of working off these feelings normally, and no one to 'strike-out' at. Unconsciously a poltergeist was created to relieve the tensions and symbolically to attack the house which they wanted to leave. It is*

not odd then that after the family had fully accepted this matter and put it into words, accepting it as the cause of the phenomena, the disturbances completely ceased."

What we think, what we feel, and what we tell ourselves manifests. Sometimes we simply don't realize that until the contrast of a negative experience comes along and shows us just that. William began to take his research outside family homes and into businesses as well, where he found the same results again and again. People who were miserable in their jobs, projecting unhappiness, feeling frustrated and who generally resided in a place of negative unhealed emotion were manifesting experiences that mirrored and often created more of the same emotion: fear, frustration, and upset. Contrast can birth discoveries, and sometimes it can uncover the gifts and abilities that you otherwise wouldn't notice.

When William shifted his attention to children, the results became that much clearer. Kids who came from what many would consider a "broken home" or who were in welfare or foster care, as well as kids who were feeling anger, frustration or hurt that was left unchecked exhibited these abilities as well. William's survey and study indicated that this kind of situation was present often in many of the 116 poltergeist cases: a third involved children under the age of nineteen who were living away from home at the time of the explosion of activity. So what happened when all of this negativity and contrast was cleaned up? Dr. Roll explained:

"... destructive only when the [agents] were in the company of individuals who seemed to arouse their anger by abuse, confine-

ment, demands and other aversive activities. But when the social environment became supportive, the nonlocal behavior [i.e., the poltergeist phenomena] occurred without destruction of property... From a psychoanalytic perspective, the destructive incidents could be considered symptoms of 'parapsychopathology,' as suggested by Rhine... But when attended by investigators who treat the [agent] with kindness and respect, the occurrences may serve as a positive mechanism to obtain attention and for the researcher to learn more about nonlocal behavior."

In short, your emotions create. You are a creator, from the very core of your being, and not just with negative experiences. Throughout the twenty years I've been a researcher and investigator, the same has proven true for clients who have come to me with wonderfully positive creations and manifestations as well. "The better it gets, the better it gets," as they say, but the filters and emotions we fail to deal with and heal seem to greatly affect physical and mental health, as well as the results we create in our day-to-day experiences. Sometimes, it is the beliefs or story we hold that dictate the results in our lives in ways our filters prevent us from seeing. What filter does well-being have to pour through to express itself *through you?* Your emotions and beliefs are doing one of two things: hindering or helping. They are either in the way of what you want, or they are aiding in what you want.

The great thing about negative emotion is that the lessons born from it are irreplaceable. We have an instinct to move towards joy, and when we aren't feeling it, we get angry. We know that's not our genuine state, just as Dr. Eben Alexander discovered with the Girl on the Butterfly Wing. But whether we see that negative emotion as an indicator and get stuck there or allow it to manifest outwards is another story. What is the contrast here to tell you? What are you giving birth to that you aren't flying with? Every subject is two subjects: the wanted and unwanted. Where are you predominantly thinking?

Psychokinesis is a wonderful gift because not only does it remind us we are indeed more than the meat suit we are walking around in, but it is a lesson in understanding our effect on the world around us. It causes us to rethink whom we're spending time with, how we're feeling, and what the dominant influences in our lives really are. It also reminds us that verbal language is not always the first currency we exchange with. While we may believe we are "putting on a face to the world," the reality is very different. Energetically, we are influencing our experience with how we think and feel constantly. Our beliefs about our world are often hindering our expression. Not the beliefs we offer to others, but the beliefs we tell ourselves in the dark of the night at 3 a.m. when no one else is around – those inner truths we may not be willing to outwardly speak. Those emotions and those beliefs find a way through.

If you're not healing the wound, you're bleeding everywhere.

It may not show up in flying objects or strange noises, but I guarantee you that if you look at your life, it's showing up somewhere: in your relationships, your job, your success level, or your bank account. With psychokinesis, many neurophysical theories have come about over the years. Why do some people manifest events in the form of bizarre phenomena, yet others may simply create events or circumstances that mimic the emotion? Roll commented, "Something else besides repressed hostility must comprise the difference between those who express this unknown via PK, and those who express themselves by normal means, and... this key difference so far eludes our psychological tests." Innumerable things have been suggested, everything from epileptic brain function, to health issues, to comas and trance episodes. There has been no conclusion reached. Monitoring of brain wave activity using electroencephalography (EEG) has often revealed no clear signs of abnormality in the agents' electro-cortical functioning during rest.

One theory posed by Roll and neurologist Elson de Montagno was that neuroelectric discharges traveling through the brainstem to the person's body (to produce muscle movements) may somehow get "blocked." Instead this energy is redirected outward into the surrounding environment to produce psychokinetic phenomena. At the end of the day, the cause is unclear, but the bottom line stays the same: Whether you're creating flying objects and bending spoons or you're creating events in your everyday life you're unhappy with, the creation begins with how you feel and how you think.

YOU GET TO CHOOSE

Don't give your mind to someone else. You are the pilot. No one has to work your job, lie in your bed, walk in your shoes, or feel how you feel. Being is an internal state: it's what matters to you and what you value. You've got to be clear about what you do, why you do it, and how you're doing it because without clarity and the suppression of your inner truth, you hinder your instinct. Clarity is a gift, and you need to be clear about what you've got going on, or else you'll end up more stuck than a pig in mud, manifesting and creating the experiences around you that you don't want, whether they be paranormal or not.

Most people have no idea why they're miserable. Have you ever noticed that? They have no clue why they're upset and mad as a wet cat. You ask them what's wrong, and they'll tell you why you're the problem – that's what happens with those who don't deal with their stuff: you become the target. What's so interesting in many of these poltergeist cases throughout history is that the activity is often directed at the person whom the individual or "agent" is pissed off with. Isn't that interesting? They feel they can't speak up, they've lost their voice, they put on a smile, yet it doesn't matter. That frustration and anger finds a way to show up regardless. See, that's how this works: you can't bury what you're feeling simply because you're not speaking it. Speaking is not the predominant language of the world we live in; it is an incredibly small factor in terms of conveying a message! You can hurt or uplift someone simply by standing in their presence with a certain energy and facial expression, and in fact, that usually means more than a positive word with a false energy. And the funny thing about these poltergeist cases is that in almost every one of them, the person the anger was directed at had absolutely no clue as to why it was happening. Not one. In fact, they blamed it on some disincarnate spirit and not the person involved.

Losing your voice not only keeps you silent, but your negative emotion doesn't convey to the other person or people that you've got a problem. In fact, most of the people who have hurt you probably don't have a damn clue, but there you are, so upset that objects are flying around the room, and your other relationships are a mess because you're hanging on to anger that doesn't even affect them! They've got no clue, and now you're just "weird"! I've had clients in these exact situations, and they were so unclear about what was going on within them emotionally, they weren't even aware they were that mad. They had lost touch with themselves on such a level that they were completely unaware they were harboring that level of discomfort in their body. Life coach and spiritual teacher Iyanla Vanzant calls this level of unawareness "neck-down dead," and it is when we become so out of touch with our own emotions that we "numb out." Negativity can get really uncomfortable, especially when we don't believe we can have different results or if we are the type of person who cannot accept we have a part to play in the reality around us. If you have it figured out that you are at the mercy of whatever happens to you, you are running your life on default, and when you couple that with not feeling you have a voice, I've got news for you: your life is about to blow up in ways you can't even see coming yet.

MANIFESTING VEGAS

"If I could really create my reality, we'd all be rich!"

We've all heard it. The age-old skeptical argument that everything happens to us, and we are at the mercy of an unpredictable and thoughtless world, and if PK was real, we'd all be swimming in money. Well, how many of you have tried it? Like *really* tried it?

Let me introduce you to Dr. Joe Gallenberger. He teaches some very important principles, and he describes three key factors he learned during two decades of what he calls "casino-PK":

- PK is real and can be taught, becoming more reliable with practice.
- Negative factors (tiredness, stress, egocentricity, caffeine and alcohol) inhibit *positive* and controlled PK expression, while positive factors (meditation, exercise and being "grounded" and open-hearted) help to facilitate it.
- Feedback needs to be immediate and clear, as is often the case in casinos.

So what in the world is casino-PK, you might ask? In short, it's learning how to create your reality... on purpose, in Vegas. You read that correctly, and it means exactly what you think it means.

Joe earned a degree in psychology in 1972 from the University of Memphis and gained a PhD in clinical psychology in 1979 from the same university, with a thesis entitled *A Comparison of Child Abusers with Members of Other Dysfunctional Families*. In 1995, he began exploring psychokinesis after achieving statistically significant results under controlled laboratory conditions, and after thirty years at the famous Monroe Institute, he decided to begin holding workshops on PK and how to use it. This included using psychokinesis in practical terms, such as winning big in Vegas casinos. In *Edgescience*, the magazine of the Society for Scientific Exploration, Gallenberger described his journey from PK lab subject to organizing group PK parties in the casino and talked about his early days at the Monroe Institute and at Princton's PEAR (Princeton Engineering Anomalies Research laboratories), training himself to influence the fall of dice under various conditions.

After a while, the labs were no longer enough. Joe began to wonder how this really applied to everyday life and if it could really be used in a way that was practical. For him, the best testing ground he could think of was the arena of gambling in Las Vegas. This was random targeted generation without the ability for him to cheat or manipulate the outcomes himself, for dice in casinos need to be as random as possible to prevent massive losses. Casinos are also highly charged and motivating environments for PK expression, rather than being stuck in the four walls of an unmotivating and sterile laboratory. Gallenberger ran ninety-nine workshops between 1999 and 2020 using dice and slot machines to teach PK, watching feat after feat of this phenomenon beat the odds of the casinos again and again.

Although people have challenged his findings that money is a good motivator for PK response, Joe is convinced that, with the right preparation, it is simply another means of bringing the spiritual to the physical. In Joe's view, money is not a "spiritual distraction" at all, as some have claimed, but rather a tool to show we really can create what we want in our life experience through the right states of consciousness.

In the end, places like the Monroe Institute, which also trained CIA agents in remote viewing during the Gateway Project in 1983, teach people to create their reality, literally. We are not separate from the events around us or the world we live in, let alone the people we meet along the way. Our driving instinct to seek joy and to daydream and to visualize is, as Albert Einstein once said, "A preview of life's coming attractions." Our job is to give ourselves a clear path to express it by tending to our own joy and our emotional center. It drives us to ask big questions and reassess our current environment if things aren't right or what we want. We tend to identify so strongly with our beliefs that admitting it needs to change becomes a crisis of identity! We fail to realize that hanging on to what is no longer serving us may indeed be the very reason you feel you're just stuck. As PK demonstrates to us again and again, we are influencing our environment and probabilities even when we don't realize we are. Nothing we think and feel goes unnoticed by the Universe; it is working in constant response to our beliefs, thoughts, projections and states of being as we move throughout our life. We are not just physical or nonphysical, we are both. One could argue that the physical is indeed the smaller part of who we are, the extension of something nonphysical entirely.

We are in a constant state of becoming, and at every moment we are sending signal after signal to the Universe and our environment, claiming the probabilities that will ultimately appear before us. We pick from the piles we like and the piles we don't like, and in the end, we tend to include a mix of all of it, wanted and unwanted. Clarity is a rare thing nowadays, and to get clear means that you're operating from a place of awareness of who you are and why you are the way you are. You're clear about any incongruence you have between what you say, what you think and the energy you present. You might not like all of it, but you've got to be clear on why you do it;

otherwise you block your ability to change the things you don't want and gain more of the things you do want. Psychokinesis is a lesson in clarity. That's it in the simplest of terms that I can come up with for you. We don't know the mechanisms that cause it to work, but I'm guessing you probably can't explain how your toaster toasts either. Guess what? You still use it! You probably can't give me the scientific definition of gravity, but you know what happens when you hit a patch of icy road and fall over! I'm guessing you don't float. We don't have to understand everything about psychokinesis, but it teaches us to be clear on our own thoughts, feelings, and actions so that we can do what we do in a manner that best serves us and those around us.

The power of our focus is unmatched. The fact we have a mind that can create and affect the environment around us is not something to be taken lightly. In order to follow our instinct, our inner guidance, we can't afford to muddy the water. We have to operate in integrity and be mindful of what we're manifesting. We can't blame our neighbor or some disincarnate spirit all the time. We can't shake our fists and say "the Universe just hates me!" We have a duty to look after the tools we have, and a mind can alter worlds in ways we have yet to fully grasp. The great thing is there is nothing you need to do to earn one; you don't need to go to school to attain a certificate to say you can use it. You already have one, primed and ready and available for you to shape, mold and hone. The question becomes: What do you choose to do with it? What do you really want, and do you love yourself enough to create it?

LESSON 9
EVERYTHING STARTS WITH A STORY

*"The canvas, which is to say the unconscious, considers the painter's
first stroke, and then tells the painter's hand how to respond to it
with a shape of a certain color and texture. And then, if all is well,
the canvas ponders this addition and comes up with further
recommendations."*
— Kurt Vonnegut

If you want to know the end, look at the beginning.

This concept has become a mantra for me in every case I've ever taken and every endeavor I embark on, not just in regard to the paranormal, but involving nearly everything I do. The energy in which something begins, including intentions and attitudes, is often indicative of the conclusion of said event. In short, if it begins with anger, underlying bad blood, frustration, hurt feelings or negative influence, odds are those broken pieces will eventually come to the surface in ways you can't always predict. By the same token, endeavors that begin with healed and whole people, and things that begin with positive potential often carry through that way, and although they might end, the ending will usually flow with the same energy that birthed its inception. Hauntings work this way as well. If you want to understand a toxic haunting, take a hard look at the people. If *you've* got some thing going on that isn't giving you the results you want, take a good look in the mirror and slap the first person you see. We may not have intentionally started it, but we always have a role to play within it, and if things are going south, the odds are you can find the roots in the beginning, even if you have to do a bit of deep digging.

It has always interested me that humans give meaning to the phenomena around us, including the paranormal kind. We touched on this in lesson 7; however, it is not just tales of monsters and mysteries in which we assign experiences and influence, it can be something as simple as experiencing a minor unexplained event and then creating connections to other things around us. I recall a case I took over a decade ago where a few fascinating incidents occurred in client's home, including the movement of objects and the manipulation of electrical devices that remained unexplained, and she then began noticing other oddities such as a funny-looking tree stump in her backyard and began connecting such a peculiarity to the movement of objects in her house. Neither had anything to do with the other, yet it becomes so easy to assign meaning and connection to the things around us when something appears to give us an explanation.

Often, these meanings are created through a number of various means and are dictated by our own beliefs and filters through which we see the world. If we are raised to believe the paranormal is evil, we will assign an evil meaning. That tree stump might be an omen of bad tidings or a "curse" on the land. If the paranormal is something positive, it might take on the meaning of a sign from the universe or a "place of healing." That being said, a pure skeptic may assign it the meaning of "nothing" or coincidence because the paranormal simply doesn't exist; that also is a meaning. For myself, I did not see the tree stump as something logically connected to anything else going on in the home or on the property, but the story that my client told herself about the stump gave it purpose and great significance.

For years, I have taught my clients one simple phrase: "I give all meaning to everything I see."

This is a powerful statement, and I encourage them, as they go through their day and experiences, to ask themselves what meaning they are giving to the experience they are currently having, paranormal or not. The meaning we assign to the day-to-day things around us and the tone in which we do so carry a great amount of weight on what energy we are bringing to the table of both the Universe and to other people. I find nothing more infuriating that trying to work with individuals who have already decided to "put their dukes up." The meaning they give to everything you say or do is usually underhanded or that you're somehow "out to get them," so they will get you first. We've all run into someone like this, and no matter what you do or say, you can't get them to budge on their erroneous belief. It's because the meaning they give to the things they experience are given through a filter of distrust, so the meaning they have chosen to assign is that whatever you did must be in effort to sabotage them somehow.

Events are neutral. Nothing is either good or bad; they are simply events in space and time. The meaning we assign to such events is what ultimately gives them significance in either a good or bad way, depending on our values, emotions, and beliefs. We usually base these assignments on our emotions and very rarely with our thinking, but once we do assign them on a thinking level, we begin to pair words with those emotions and thoughts. Words are very powerful because they are the first physical manifestation of emotion into our environment. Speaking can turn something from energy in our mind to a reality in our life in very short order, and when we don't mind our mouth, our speaking can create things we may not intend. That being said, we can also speak words that, with the proper intention, can move mountains. Even the word *incantation* comes directly from the Latin word *incantare,* "enchant." *Incantare* itself has *cantare* as a root, reminding us this dates back as far as the fourteenth century and that words are often used in ritual magic or other practices. Even the childhood word of "abracadabra" translates to "I create what I speak."

The illusory truth effect (also known as the illusion of truth, validity effect, truth effect, or the reiteration effect) describes how, when we hear the same false information repeated again and again, we often come to believe it is true. We've experienced this in a plethora of ways since 2019 when social media became a quagmire of pandemic information and a tool of misinformation on behalf of both sides of the political coin. We may have scrolled through our news feed and noticed a story on occasion, but the more we were exposed to that story, the more it began to seem normal and true, and our pre-existing knowledge can't prevent this. We like to think that a few searches and our already substantial base of knowledge would guard us from these fallacies, right? Well, not so much.

To make sense of the world and to find "shortcuts" through all the 35,000 or more decisions we need to make every day, we use something called heuristics: basic strategies that allow for generalizations, or rules of thumb, reduce cognitive load, and can be effective for making immediate judgments. One particular type of heuristic is known as the Availability Heuristic. This can lead to bad decision-making because memories that are easily recalled are frequently insufficient for figuring out how likely things are to happen again in the future. It means that what we speak and expose ourselves to really does matter and not just in the short term. This can actually affect how we draw conclusions and therefore how we speak about the world as well as how we speak over it.

THE CURSED CABINET

In 2001 in Portland, Oregon, a fellow by the name of Kevin Mannis was seeking out furniture at yard sales for his furniture restoration company. He owned a little hole-in-the-wall business in Burnside Bridge, and as he was shopping, he came across an old cabinet. It looked all in one piece but could use a slight bit of fixing up, so he purchased it and got to talking with the young lady hosting the yard sale. As a furniture restorer and history buff, he wanted to know where it came from and what journeys it had taken. As it turned out, the young lady was the granddaughter of a recently deceased Holocaust survivor named Havela, who escaped Nazi-occupied Poland. Her family was tragically murdered by the Nazi occupation, and she, in turn, fled to Spain to escape them. When Havela moved courageously to the United States, the small wine cabinet was the only thing she took with her.

As Mannis paid for the cabinet, the girl said, "Oh, I see you bought the dybbuk box!" Unfamiliar with the term, Mannis inquired, and the young lady went on to explain that her grandmother had been diligent about keeping the cabinet locked away. In Jewish lore, dybbuk boxes served as homes for evil spirits and should not be tampered with. She quickly informed him that the box should never be opened, and if he dared to disobey, his life would never be the same again. Mannis dismissed the story and immediately took the box back to his shop for restoration as a gift, and upon opening it, he discovered a few odd items: two US wheat pennies dating to 1925 and 1928, two locks of hair, a dried rosebud, a four-legged candlestick, a golden wine cup, and a granite sculpture inscribed with the Hebrew word *shalom*. The Shema, a Jewish prayer, was carved in the back of the box itself. Then, on Halloween in 2012, he passed the box to his mother as a gift. In an episode of *Paranormal Witness*, his mother described the box as having a feeling of pure evil coming out of it, but it didn't end there.

Soon, Mannis' family began to complain about the box, and over the course of two years, strange things allegedly happened, including the doors opening and closing by themselves, horrible smells coming from the open doors, recurring nightmares of a woman with sunken eyes, and the brother of a shop employee committing suicide after knocking the box off a shelf by accident. Within a couple of years, the employee himself also committed suicide. When Mannis tried to pawn the box off on his girlfriend, she claimed she began seeing "shadow figures," and Mannis felt he had no other choice but to list it on eBay and hope for the best.

His description of the box was long and detailed, ensuring he included every last piece of the story he could remember in a "buyer beware" statement. He concluded it with a spine-chilling phrase: "Help me."

It sold, and reports began circulating about the dybbuk box and its nightmarish qualities. Incidents from buyers included choking attacks, strange bleeding, and recurring dreams of a creepy old woman, to name a few. Even the singer Post Malone claimed he had frightening encounters with the box once it was in the hands of entertainer Zak Bagans, who grabbed it up for his haunted museum attraction in Las Vegas and featured it on a number of *Ghost Adventure* episodes. He claimed to audience members again and again that this was a demon-haunted box with a history of terror befalling anyone who owned it. His film crew claimed they saw a figure manifesting inside the box although the cameras captured nothing. In the ensuing months of his encounter, Post Malone stated his home was broken into and his plane needed to make an emergency landing, and not long after that, he was involved in a car wreck. All of these incidents he attributed to the encounter with the dybbuk box.

The media exploded with fascination around this strange cabinet, and two movies were born from the stories. But the reports didn't stop there. More owners came forward claiming they were having strange misfortunes ever since owning the cursed cabinet, but things began unraveling in 2021 when journalist Charles Moss interviewed both Mannis and the second owner, a man named Haxton, for *Input Magazine*. In it, Moss wrote:

> *"Though both Mannis and Haxton received money from their work on* The Possession, *Haxton seems to have benefitted the most from the Dybbuk Box, financially and publicity-wise. He's considered the expert on the subject, partly because he had it the longest out of all its owners, partly because he wrote the book, and partly because he's made himself so available for media appearances. Jason was very Johnny-on-the-spot to make money off of it.*
>
> *"Haxton, whom I've spoken to on the phone and emailed with quite a bit, has some criticism of his own for Mannis. 'I think Kevin was shocked because though he might've come up with the idea and the concept, he would have never gotten the book written,' Haxton says. 'He never finishes anything. He would have never gotten the movie done. I got red carpet treatment and everything. I was with the stars, and he was the background noise. And it probably pissed him off. But that's the way it is.' Mannis, for his part, denies that the fame surrounding Haxton's book and public appearances ever bothered him."*

Finally, the truth about the dybbuk box was finally confessed in a conversation between Mannis and Moss in a second interview. Charles Moss pulled no punches and called Mannis on what he suspected was an elaborate lie, and Mannis owned up quickly, stating that the dybbuk box eBay listing was, indeed, a well-written hoax. He stated to Moss:

"I am a creative writer. The Dybbuk Box is a story that I created. And the Dybbuk Box story has done exactly what I intended it to do when I posted it 20 years ago... Which is to become an interactive horror story in real-time."

He went on to state that the box did indeed come from a yard sale, however no holocaust survivors were involved, and the original owner was an attorney.

"The carving in the back of it is my carving. The stone that was in the box is something that is a signature creation of mine also. Make no mistake, I conceived of the Dybbuk Box – the name, the term, the idea – and wrote this creative story around it to post on eBay."

Taking the investigation further, Moss interviewed two of Mannis' close friends, one who confessed that the hair "found" in the box upon its opening was actually his own. They also praised their friend for being a brilliant storyteller and that the motivation behind the prank was actually due to relationship issues Mannis had been experiencing with his girlfriend. Angry and frustrated, he decided to put his energy elsewhere and create one of the most elaborate hoaxes in recent history.

So what about that heart-stopping interview Ida, his own mother, gave on *Paranormal Witness*? Well, it was an Oscar-worthy performance and a bit of "motherly support," as Mannis called it, and in order to keep it going, he kept adding new details into the public's attention through shows and entertainers such as Zak Bagans, who continued to feature it on his show and in his attractions. Kevin Mannis stated: "The only way to regain control and to have viable assets was to keep writing the story."

And write he did. So much so, Bagans has not been able to let it go, claiming that the story must indeed be real – perhaps because he invested so much time into it?

Either way, the legend of the cursed cabinet continues and leaves little doubt that a good story coupled with a great *storyteller* is a powerful tool.

You are your greatest storyteller. You are telling yourself a narrative, true or untrue, every moment of every second of every minute of every day. That being said, it is easy to have others slip into that narrative as well: parents, peers, friends, and bosses. Who are you allowing to write your narrative? When we don't have a handle on who we are, it becomes easy for others to influence that narrative for us. Who we spend our time around influences our story, and sometimes, that influence can become an echo chamber of beliefs that don't serve us. In the world of parapsychology, beliefs and the stories we tell ourselves influence our interpretation of the world around us in innumerable ways, and what we tell ourselves ultimately determines our interactions with both this physical world we can see, hear, taste and touch, and the nonphysical world as well. Statistically, nonbelievers and people who are less open-minded towards paranormal events score poorly in experiments like remote viewing, as we talked about in the first lessons. This isn't because they are less apt to have the skill, it is because we tend to believe the stories we tell ourselves and sometimes even the stories we offer to others.

I have often kept this motto close at hand: "If I want my life to have a new meaning, I have to give meaning to that."

Just as it is true that we give meaning to "cursed" objects or places where we believe a paranormal event ought to have happened, we can also give it a new meaning and have a new experience. This can also be true of people who have had a traumatic experience in their lives and have associated it with a day or a place. Reframing and reassigning new meaning to that day can create a world of difference in the healing of our psyche and emotions. Rather than continuing to validate a story, collecting our own data and reframing the experience can be the key to clarity.

When we get bogged down with the wrong story, we begin asking the wrong questions. Had we been given the true story behind the notorious dybbuk box from the beginning, the questions and experiences surrounding it would almost be guaranteed to be quite different. Perhaps instead of asking "What is haunting this object?" we would have been far more curious as to what drove a person to create the story to begin with, and this would have been a very different tale altogether. Putting forward the proper information and taking stock of said information is a process, and it is crucial in parapsychology if you want to get to the bottom of an experience or haunted tale; however, it is also a critical thinking skill that reaches far beyond the paranormal. This ability is crucial to instinct, and the wrong story can have the ability to hinder our internal guidance if we aren't careful. This is where emotions and thinking really become intertwined because in order to unravel a narrative, especially our own, instinct is a much-needed factor. How it feels and the data collected about the facts both need to be considered heavily, and this isn't always an easy process. Judgments and predetermined stories and old filters can get in the way, such as negative associations or past upsets.

Sometimes, other people can be indicative of a problem, as mentioned above, but just like negative entities can be indicators of unbalance and upset, so can the living! If one person tells you something you might not want to hear, you don't have to listen. If three unrelated people tell you the same thing, something is up, and you need to unpack that. Don't tell yourself a story that's not true just to make it fit into the narrative you've got going about who you are or what's happening; be willing to weigh the evidence. If you don't, you can get washed up the wrong river, asking the wrong questions, and beating the wrong drum before you know it! It's hard to unring a bell, and many times, this is when people begin acting like they know what's up when they really don't and end up out of order as hell. You can talk yourself *into* trouble, and usually, when we talk ourselves *out* of trouble, it is often because we've talked ourselves into it first.

Stories remind us to become mindful about what we're speaking to ourselves as well as others. In 2001, on the fateful day of September 11, the devastation in New York when the Twin Towers fell rocked the foundations of everyone who witnessed the event. What many don't know is that the Parapsychology Foundation's Lisette Coly was flooded with calls that day. Each emotional and terrified caller was seeking counsel because they had believed that their likely deceased loved one who had plummeted to their death or was, perhaps, caught in a burning inferno would become "stuck" after death, left to torment, because that's what many television shows and popular culture often perpetuate. Overwhelmed with desperate people, it fell on the Parapsychology Foundation to dismantle this barrage of misinformation and elevated the need for proper information to be disseminated to the public about actual parapsychological discoveries and survival after death research. Upon talking to Lisette Coly during an episode of my podcast *Supernatural Circumstances*, the phrase "do no harm" was placed on the table, and rightly so. Of what harm or benefit is your story? How do you tell your story, and how does it impact others around you, or have you thought about it? Is your story burying your gifts in a flood of "I'm not good enough," or are you telling a story that is creating meaningful experiences in your life? Are you throwing a negative shade on an experience that might not be as you label it?

In short, *How do you tell your story?*

WHO'S TELLING YOUR STORY? THE SLENDER MAN EFFECT

It's a big question and one most people are utterly unaware of until they are asked to write it down and read it back. Whether you're creating a story about a cursed cabinet or about your own life, stories have a way of snowballing into real effects, and the more often a story is told, the more concrete it becomes. It's amazing to me how stories born of creativity, basic perception, and on occasion outright lies, can begin to change the way our minds perceive the world around us. There have been many such cases over the years such as the internet sensation of Slender Man, a character created by Eric Knudsen as an online horror trope for the *Something Awful* online forums contest, which soon became the center of a horrific murder in the United States. Something that began as a fictional romp was spun in the minds of two young children until they attempted to sacrifice their young friend by stabbing her nineteen times in attempts to appease the spirit of Slender Man, who in their minds had become quite real.

People have now reported seeing a representation or apparition of a similar figure throughout the years and have said on many occasions that these spiritual monsters are indeed very real and not a work of fiction at all. Some have even made the argument that the creature was actually drawn because the image of Slender Man has existed in various shapes and forms far beyond the creation of an internet photoshop image. The character designer has maintained that it was his own creation and that Slender Man was nothing more than a drawing, but for the two twelve-year-old girls, Anissa Weier and Morgan Geyser, in Waukesha, Wisconsin, United States, Slender Man was as real as the friend they lured to her near-death. In this particular case, mental illness proved a factor in Geyser, yet not in Weier. While Geyser felt no empathy, Weier was described as feeling guilty for stabbing the victim, but felt that the attack was needed to appease Slender Man. While this is a pretty extreme case, the power of the stories we tell is illustrated.

Losing our bead on instinct and our connection with our own guidance system can cause us to miss opportunities and, in some cases, pull us way off track. When we aren't in touch with our own story and allow others to pull us into their own, we can lose our way and find ourselves in situations far greater than what we could have imagined. Now, hopefully that won't mean you find yourself on trial for murder next to a schizophrenic counterpart, but the wrong story with the wrong people can really throw you off in the ditch. That being said, the right story will take us where we can only begin to imagine.

As I have mentioned before, a deliberate story has a way of playing itself out in the world. Like a script from a film director, when we outline a story for our life that is directed around what we really want, things have a way of coming to fruition in ways we can't imagine. When we begin to put an image out to the world in words, our experience has the opportunity to structure opportunities for us in ways that truly blow our minds. Think about it: the power of writing has the ability to inspire, pass down traditions, educate, record events and to pass down reasoning. If you want to experience how someone thinks, take a look at what they write or journal! We pass information to others through writing, but we also affirm it with ourselves, and whatever we affirm with ourselves will eventually become a believable idea. Repetition is powerful, and what we repeat and entrench in our minds resonates in our being. We marinate in our stories because we repeat them through our thoughts and emotions so often throughout our day in ways we aren't often aware of. We marinate in the energy we speak, and without the awareness of that projection and its implications, we lose touch with the instinct that can guide us to what we really want in our life experience.

Writing and storytelling is perhaps one of the most prolific ways we pass on ideas; however, the emotions we choose to have around those stories is up to us. The breakdown for most people is that they will often have an emotion around a story that may not serve them. We don't have to engage in every piece of information we receive, nor do we have to participate in the story being told to us. As an investigator and researcher, this is invaluable to me, and it is a trait we must learn to understand and use. Getting pulled into the interpretation of a frightening haunting by a client can cause us to close off information or potential causes and problematic factors that are needed to put the pieces together correctly. Being pulled into someone else's interpretation and storytelling can cause us to not only negate our own instinct, but begin to believe in a story that only has its basis in personal filters rather than facts. How we respond and react to the stories others tell is crucial in keeping our own personal and emotional balance, and what's more, knowing how we react is just as important.

Have you ever found yourself online wishing you could scream at a commenter on social media? Or maybe you've taken that extra step and have already been sucked in to a nonsense commentary where neither one of you came out on top. Have you ever noticed that, in those situations, people are usually not prepared to change the story they're telling? Instead, they are there to defend it, like robbers blockading their hold. Everyone is usually on the defense, and most of the time, no mind is changed by the time hours are wasted frantically typing and posting. Stories have a way of rooting us in dysfunction if we aren't carefully telling the right ones, and nothing pulls us in faster to someone else's dysfunction than hurt, fear or frustration. How many times have you been online and have positively ranted about something wonderful? Probably not that many.

In cases like Slender Man, fear is the motivator, and fear sells faster than almost anything else on the planet – or so it is believed. The more frightening the tale, the more it enthralls us, which is why the jump-scare ghost-hunting shows of today do so incredibly well. You can't turn on the Travel Channel or T+E networks anymore without finding at least a few of them airing every day. Those are all fun and games for entertainment, but what we're internalizing matters. The story we tell ourselves about the things we observe in our day-to-day experience literally changes our experience in how we think, feel, and vibrate.

~

LANGUAGE & THE ARGUMENT FOR A CONSCIOUS UNIVERSE

"Consciousness has a lot going for it as a candidate for a new terminology of transcendence. Unlike the term God, we know it refers to something real – inescapably and fundamentally so. In contrast, the notion of God has become a dubious idea, and is too often used as part of the vocabulary of political oppression if not outright murder and empire." – Michael Grosso

Nowhere is storytelling more prominent than in the texts and scripts of religion, and nowhere does language carry as much weight, controversy and baggage. For many, even the idea of a word like "God" either frightens, angers, or inspires people all over the globe. Words can unite us or drive a wedge between us in misunderstanding or judgment. Today, many people will often say, "I am spiritual, not religious." What that usually entails is "I don't go to church or practice doctrine from a text, but I believe that there is a conscious force in the universe, and I am a part of something larger than me." Where religion is associated with dogma and practice, spiritual people don't feel a need to rely on anything external to assist them on their life journey. The need for religion in today's world continues to thin, but the needs of finding happiness, answering the big questions of life and the universe, as well as looking for that spiritual "something" still remains.

The baggage that has been wrapped around religion and its commentary is often well deserved. It doesn't take a historian to look back on the not-so-distant past and see the chaos and hurt many organizations have inflicted on various groups of people throughout the years. However, when we begin replacing trigger words such as God with something like "consciousness," this new language can have the power to open up a new discussion. Words matter, and when you have a distinction as important as "spiritual" versus "religious," one can really see the strength in how terminology and how we tell our story is perceived and how it impacts those around us. A spiritual person might say something like "I believe in consciousness," and that may have a lot to do with the fact that consciousness isn't something we struggle to discover. There's no great hunt for consciousness as there often is for "God"; we all rest in our own consciousness, and we all know we are indeed conscious. In fact, most of the great religions point to an underlying consciousness of some sort, and it is a connecting factor within and throughout all of them.

What we are experiencing is viewing the world through the lens of different language and how we perceive each of the words we use is important to be aware of. Even around our words, we tell a story. Those words can incite emotion or, depending on the story you've told around such vocabulary, shut down a mind or heart in a simple sentence. But how you receive words is just as important. How you receive those stories and the filters with which we process them is something worth examination. It is often said "you can't push a person's buttons unless they are already preinstalled," and that is ever so true in relationship to spirituality and religion. Very rarely do people sit in a gray area around either idea, and it can prove a hot-button topic to avoid at the family gatherings! It demonstrates, however, how our filters really work and can be an indicator to us of the stories that are either serving us or causing breakdown between others and within ourselves. If you want to really get an understanding of where you're hurting, think about the things that send you off the rails and, rather than asking if it is true, ask yourself what you're telling yourself about that subject. The answers are quite enlightening.

Asking whether the story you've written for yourself is true can cause your defeat before you even get off the ground. We often have factors within the stories we tell that we feel are factual and true for us, but the question of whether the flavor or essence of the story serves our greater good and higher calling is another matter. The wrong story can kill your instinct. If you aren't rooting for you, then no one else will either. Understanding our story and the whys and hows of what we do and why we do it can stop us from being pulled off the main road when an untruth comes along that doesn't fit in our ear very well. It keeps us steady and stable when harsh critics, bullies, hoaxers, and negative or ill-intentioned people come our way. When we know our story and ensure that what we speak is in alignment with our integrity and our purpose, it becomes much easier to receive the inspiration of instinct and know when to make the right move. How we speak and act is a demonstration of the stories we tell about who we are, what we do, and the baggage we haven't yet let go of. Your story is powerful because it is the basis of all thought and information you filter. Whatever you haven't healed will shape and structure the sound of your story, the actions you choose and the results in your life. Our vocabulary shapes our reality, and we are the greatest storytellers in our individual lifetimes. How you master that art is entirely up to you, but never forget the impact and ripple effect you alone create in the world. You matter. Your story matters. What you speak matters. How will you write yours?

LESSON 10
DREAM THE IMPOSSIBLE, YOU JUST MIGHT GET IT

"If parapsychology deals with all the personality manifestations that are beyond explanation by physics, then by definition it should claim the entire spiritual order of reality."
—J. B. Rhine

The idea that our brains are simply broadcasting and receiving stations, rather than the source of emerging consciousness, is not a product of recent thoughts. David Chalmers, noted philosopher, dubbed it the Hard Problem: is consciousness fundamental or emergent?

When we focus our minds or we have an idea, is it really our idea, or are we picking up something in an infinite universe of possibilities and translating a version of probable reality?

As discussed earlier around the concept of remote viewing, we have the capability of receiving images, thoughts, and ideas from outside sources and turning them into physical reality – and not just in tightly controlled labs and in relationship to espionage or zener cards. Thoughts become things, and it is the groundwork for abilities such as psychokinesis and some avenues of extrasensory perception. What we believe, how we feel, and what we focus upon can manifest in some strange and unexplainable ways; however, this information has been spread across intertwining systems of knowledge and understanding along the way. However, the one bright red thread that I have come to understand throughout my two decades in parapsychology is this: if the inspiration can be received *by* you, the universe has the ability to deliver it *through* you. In short, dream the impossible because you just might get it.

Do you remember the moment when you, in your infant studies of the paranormal and psychic abilities, realized that it wasn't all parlor tricks and magic? I do. Do you remember when you had the "aha! moment" that this wasn't all fairy tales and ghost stories? Maybe it was an experience you had or a book you read or, like J. B. Rhine, a speaker you heard. I remember mine: It was watching Loyd Auerbach and Kerry Gaynor discussing cases of spontaneous phenomena on the show *Sightings* back in the 1980s. I remember it vividly, and I also remember the wonder, magic, and the awareness of "something more" that I felt when I was listening to them. Little did I know then that this information applied to the whole of life. It was so much bigger than a ghost story or a moving object with no explanation; it was the blueprint of how our world works and how we function within the realms of creating it. It also implied something massive: that we are responsible for the probabilities we receive, and our minds have the potential to shape it as we want to see it. We don't have to create by default, responding only to situations with unchecked emotion. We can create by honing our emotions: don't bend the spoon; bend the space around the spoon.

Sounds like science fiction? Well, art tends to imitate life and vice versa. In early letters to J. B. Rhine, Carl Jung, the Swiss psychiatrist, implored Rhine to look at his ESP studies with new eyes. He suggested, as Rhine began to report on his studies of extrasensory perception, that he pay attention to a factor he felt was absolutely key in understanding how our minds have a physical effect on objects of matter. Not only that, but he suggested the relationship between the results and what was manifesting had a good deal to do with the state of being of the participant and suggested that nothing that was happening in the lab was random chance at all.

"... Nevertheless, it must be remembered that with Rhine the first series of experiments generally produced the best results, which then quickly fell off. But when it was possible to arouse a new interest in the essentially rather boring experiment, the results improved again. If follows from this that the emotional factor plays an important role."
— *The Letters of Carl Jung*

Carl Jung focused much of his career on a concept he called *synchronicity*. It makes an extraordinary claim about reality – events may be linked in diverse and strange ways that defy all physical law, causality and common sense. What would it mean if events may relate to each other only by some kind of meaning, however obscure, not by some kind of physical interaction? J. B. Rhine was hesitant about applying the concept to his work because in the infant stages, little was known to validate Jung's idea. Quantum entanglement and non-locality, which ignores spatial separation, was not widely understood at the time of Rhine. Now it is the basis for quantum cryptography and understanding particle superposition worldwide. While we have no evidence we can transmit information this way, we do know that using classical channels and through signaling and correlating, you can *affect* meaningful information.

A great example is this: Let's say you have a sick friend. If you were to "pray" a strong intentional prayer or focus that intention back in time to when they were well, could you help them move into a future where they get to wellness quicker? There is evidence that yes, you actually can. Intention, as it turns out, is a psychic phenomenon not locked into space and time. So, just like in the first chapters when we talked about sending imagery or information to someone in a ganzfeld experiment or in a remote viewing situation, intention is considered very similar.

To understand how any of this works, we have to look at the current scientific worldview, which is materialism: You are a meat machine, and that's it. Your sense of self is an illusion generated by your brain and nothing more, meaning that consciousness is emergent.

~

WITHIN SCIENCE there is a hierarchy of disciplines:

Psychology
Biology/neuroscience
Chemistry
Physics

And yes, physics is at the bottom with consciousness some-where in the neuroscience/biological ether. With this current worldview, the idea we can manifest and turn thoughts to things is impossible; it makes no sense whatsoever. Conscious-ness, your sense of awareness, then emerges out of all of that. With this ideal, consciousness must be composed of matter and energy, making it emergent. This doesn't support manifes-tation at all: How would thought ever affect any of this? Chem-istry and physics, maybe. But thought existing outside the physical body? Not with this model!

Over the last number of years, there has been a fair amount of evidence that says this is worldview may be flawed, and not in the way you might be thinking. Materialism brought us out of medieval times and has advanced science in a miraculous number of ways, so we can't knock materialism in the least. However, when you begin to dig to the bottom of many of the new problems facing scientists today in regard to conscious-ness and the big questions, something is missing. Because other phenomena like psychic phenomena are real, this throws a pretty big wrench in things when it comes to understanding many of the new results of psi experiments, which now must be considered.

Materialism has only been around about four hundred

years. When we look back further, shamanism, Hermeticism, Gnosticism, yoga, the Vedas, Buddhism and more all have a basic understanding that consciousness is fundamental to the universe.

In the perennial worldview, the philosophical tradition of the world's great thinkers from Plato, Aristotle, and Aquinas, as well as more modern thinkers such as Aldous Huxley, the idea of fundamental consciousness is introduced. In this scenario, consciousness is more dominant in the hierarchy than not. So essentially, the concept of fundamental consciousness is simple, and it has nothing to do with completely altering the current hierarchy of science. All we do is change where it falls within that hierarchy.

Consciousness
Psychology
Biology/neuroscience
Chemistry
Physics

Nothing else changes in materialism, rather materialism is just a piece of the whole, and from it emerges the world as we experience it. Consciousness becomes primary over physics, therefore allowing space for thoughts becoming things.

What we used to think was fundamental in some areas is no longer the case. Science is making progressive and at times "quantum leaps" with new information every day into areas that seem unlikely, initially "unscientific," and incredible. The leading edge of science now embraces thought leaders who would have been thought crazy years ago, and yet our view of

THE GIFT OF INSTINCT

the world we live in must begin to evolve with these new discoveries.

"I believe that consciousness is a fundamental, elementary, property of living matter. It can't be derived from anything else." – Dr. Christof Koch, neuroscientist

If that is true, then affirmations and imposing affirmations become plausible.

We have a model in our mind of the world that helps us to make sense of it. We don't get something from nothing. So where does the model come from? In my opinion and the opinion of others such as Dr. Lothar Schafer, a quantum chemist from the University of Arkansas, as well as Stuart Hameroff and Roger Penrose, it comes out of the nonempirical realm. It actualizes in thoughts in our minds, in events, and things, and it is not impossible the two are connected.

The way many see the world right now is that our current knowledge is information in a vessel: you. In ancient times, however, Indian texts such as the Vedas described it as a light, something that was all encompassing that everyone had access to. Here, all the probabilities and knowledge were already in existence; every thought that had ever been thought was still energetically available to those ready and willing to access it. This understanding of a fundamental consciousness that holds information in various forms is not a new one, and though we cannot prove something in the nonempirical world, the idea has become a strong part of the beliefs of many quantum physicists and parapsychologists alike.

So why can't we just access everything? Why can't we

manifest a myriad of probabilities where everything we want, including all the right information, just shows up? Well, the idea is that knowledge can be uncovered but only by the prepared mind. What is that, you might ask? It's exactly what we talked about in previous chapters: the preparation period. You can't uncover something totally disconnected from your model of the world and how it functions; there has to be an expansion. What you can uncover will be related to what you already know and, moreover, what you already *believe*. Without preparation, you can't find it, and some would say it can't find *you*.

The logical mind has to structure the information it possesses, and it can only do that through gradual enlargement and expansion of our thinking, so something that doesn't conform to your vision of how the world works gets projected onto what you know. It may make sense later, but at the time it may seem like one great big strange occurrence.

Is there meaning in everything? Well, is there? We assign meaning to our lives, as we spoke about before, and many times, what can seem like a random event to one, someone else may not find it random at all. Also, as we focus within certain emotional moods, outcomes seem to be directly affected. This is where our intuition and instinct begin to play a significant role. As we've talked about, intuition doesn't work in a linguistic fashion. You grasp it eventually through language, but it begins as instinct and emotion. As Scott Rogo and William Roll both argued: psi and psychokinesis are highly tied to the emotional state; the exact notion pointed out by Carl Jung in his letters regarding the work of J. B. Rhine. The physical cosmos may well be a projection of this reality; it is not tied to space and time. The reality is as small as you can think, and as large as you can think.

THE COSMIC PHILOSOPHERS

"Man moves in a world that is nothing more or less than his consciousness objectified."
  – Neville Goddard

There were plenty of people who had their eyes on J. B. Rhine's research as his experiments on the far-reaching effects of the mind and consciousness began to take hold. For over thirty years, Rhine and his lab colleagues corresponded with Einstein and Jung and celebrities such as Jackie Gleason. The Rockefeller Foundation, Alfred P. Sloan (of General Motors and Sloan-Kettering fame) and the military provided support. Even the CIA bought ESP cards from him and in the 1980s began serious exploration into these ideas with the Monroe Institute and a project known as the Gateway Experience. With all this scientific interest in the labs and remarkable results, another set of eyes had also settled intently on the notion that our mind can create our experience: Napoleon Hill.

When people think of the paranormal, Napoleon Hill is not a name that initially comes to mind. In fact, he is mostly known for his famous and revered work, *Think and Grow Rich*, originally published in 1937. In it, Hill talks about the lessons imparted to him by people like Andrew Carnegie, J. P. Morgan, and other wealthy moguls who all had one consistent message:

you create your reality with your thought. Seeking to understand how our intention and focus could create or attract the probabilities in which we experience in the physical world, Hill kept a close watch on J. B. Rhine's research and studied Rhine's work in detail, publishing a number of pages on it in his famous works. Even then, the work and goings-on at Duke University were becoming known in circles of new thinkers who were willing to push the boundaries of science and apply it to what they knew to be true: thoughts become things. Neville Goddard, Ralph Waldo Emerson, and even the likes of Albert Einstein vocalized their strong belief that imagination "is the preview of life's coming attractions."

Neville is perhaps one of the most fascinating and mysterious of this ever-growing collective of scientists, philosophers, businessmen and parapsychologists who are leaning towards this new reality. Nearly forty years after his death, Neville's words have been preserved in both books and audio recordings on every platform imaginable, and to this day, they carry great weight. From the 1930s to 1972, writing under the pen name "Neville," Goddard spoke with ease and openness about his own findings as he journeyed to understand consciousness and our own psychic abilities. He was perhaps the last century's most intellectually substantive and most passionate lecturer of the philosophy generally called New Thought. Neville was clear and concise about what he knew to be true: everything you see and experience, including other people, is the result of your own thoughts and emotional states. In short, he believed the human imagination is God, and when you understand it, the potentials and probabilities that open up for you are infinite. Even today, Neville's reputation is growing as his teachings on fundamental consciousness are found to coincide with key issues in today's quantum physics debate.

After decades of study, Goddard believed that one particular factor was responsible for manifestation: emotion. He developed a concept I still use today, which he called "thinking from the end." With this process, he believed that thinking, feeling and acting as if the event has already occurred will begin to bring forth the probability in which it actually *has*. He also believed the Scripture was wrought with examples of so-called miracles that may have been simply an extension of this same process. In an example from his 1941 book *Your Faith Is Your Fortune*, he examines the tale of Lot's wife, who turns into a pillar of salt after looking back upon the city of Sodom: "Not knowing that consciousness is ever out-picturing itself in conditions round about you, like Lot's wife you continually look back upon your problem and again become hypnotized by its seeming naturalness."

Neville believed that Christ himself was nothing more than a fictional master psychologist created to demonstrate the power of creative thought. He went on to say:

"The Bible has no reference at all to any person who ever existed, or any event that ever occurred upon earth. All the stories of the Bible unfold in the minds of the individual man."

Neville Goddard walked his walk just as well as he spoke it, and he became a noted lecturer in New York's Greenwich Village in front of packed audiences. His bold claims, such as his family's restaurant success in Barbados and manifesting a military discharge, all the way to his studies with a mystical teacher from the islands named Abdullah, were all backed up with public records. The only one lost was his military documents, which were confirmed by the army to have been destroyed in a fire.

So does it work? If you believe it, and if you believe you can have it, and then live as if you do, can you obtain it? And if so, why isn't everyone doing this? Well, the answer may be found in the same place I have found my own answers to this question when I'm dealing with a client's haunted home. In *The Romance of Metaphysics*, the occult philosopher Israel Regardie wrote:

> "Neville's method is sound enough. But the difficulty is that few people are able to muster up this emotional exaltation or this intellectual concentration which are the royal approaches to the citadel of the Unconscious. As a result of this definite lack of training or technique, the mind wanders all over the place, and a thousand and one things totally unrelated to 'I AM' are ever before their attention."

In case you missed it, you can only attract what your mind is *prepared* for. Remember that little tidbit? But what else made Neville so adept at manifesting and honing these abilities? Regardie had a theory, which I personally believe and have found myself to be correct. He stated:

> "Neville knows the art of relaxation instinctively. He is a dancer, and a dancer must, of necessity, relax. Hence I believe he does not fully and consciously realize that the average person in his audi-

ence does not know the mechanism of relaxation, does know how to 'let go.'"

Neville's message has coalesced with current debates in quantum physics, especially in the area of the "quantum measurement problem." This is a problem in particle physics where, in eighty years of laboratory experiments, it has been shown that atomic-scale particles appear in a given place only when a measurement is made. Quantum theory holds that no measurement means *no precise and localized object* anywhere on the atomic scale. In quantum data, it shows that a subatomic particle literally occupies an infinite number of places (a state called "superposition." Imagine spinning a coin with an infinite number of sides) until observation manifests it in one place. Your observation and focus is the *only* thing that makes that spinning probability a reality. In quantum mechanics, an observer's conscious decision to look or not look actually deter-mines what will show up, begging the question: What are *you* giving your attention to? What you focus on, you create.

Just as quantum physicists now believe, infinite potentials all exist at one time. It is the dominant feeling and focus you have that brings it into existence and determines the outcome. For example, if I have a client experiencing paranormal phenomenon that's less than what they want or is outright frightening, I can guarantee you that there is an emotional breakdown occurring somewhere else in their experience, and the activity has become a manifestation or mirror of a deeper-set problem. Just in the same way people who experience extremely fun and positive psychic phenomenon have a mirrored experience for the positive as well, it can happen at all levels of our emotional spectrum.

> *"Change your conception of yourself and you will automatically change the world in which you live. Do not try to change people; they are only messengers telling you who you are. Revalue yourself and they will confirm the change."*
> – Neville Goddard, Your Faith Is Your Fortune.

You may not have been focusing on the specific outcome of a haunted home, but remember: this is about receiving *probabilities*, and those probabilities will mirror the *essence* of what you've got going on internally. Like a radio dial tuner, everything you emotionally tune into will attract on that frequency. You can't get a country station on a rock n' roll station, you've got to change the dial. Want different results? **Create from the end**. How would it feel to have what you want *now*? It's not what you want that you attract, it's what you *believe to be true*.

THE GREAT TEACHER OF UPLIFTING

The paranormal and the study of parapsychology have one great thread that runs through many of its facets: it is a teacher of uplifting. It puts the power back in the hands of the person rather than ripping it away, as much of the media and horror films would have us believe. It has a miraculous way to support the evidence of your alignment with your inner world and illustrates the power and reach of imagination. Once we can truly understand that our focus creates our reality, it puts us back in the driver's seat of both parapsychology and our everyday experience with our own goals and dreams. It is a reality check that asks us loud and boldly: what patterns are holding you up?

Take your mental inventory. Now that you know that what you speak, think, and feel impact your world, take a rock-solid inventory of how you're presenting into the world. I'm not talking physical appearance; I mean what are you presenting energetically, verbally, emotionally to the consciousness around you? If you're not sure, one of the best ways to tell is to examine what has already manifested in your life. Reverse engineer your current world, and much will be explained; at least, that's what I've discovered.

One of the most wonderful things about this aspect of the paranormal is that it gets us picky about our thinking and our environment. It teaches selfishness in the best way possible: be self-full. No one else has to see your vision, and you don't need other people's agreement with you in order to create going forward. This is your vision, your dream, your path, and you get to carve it out in the exact way you wish. Never judge your clarity on how others respond because nothing will throw you right off track than when you are not settled into your vision and Aunt Mavis comes along and tells you why you were never that good at something! Or your teacher says you couldn't amount to anything. They can't see your dream because they are not you. They cannot share your perspective no matter how hard they might try, and it's no fault of theirs! Your point of awareness in the universe is unique, and only you can tell that story in a way that matters to you. You get to determine the "what" and the "why," and in fact, the "why" is usually the best thing to focus on. Why you want something is usually far easier to find joy in than even the "what." Parapsychology is a bit like this as well: the "what" is usually quite obvious, and the "why" is the journey.

Here's where it gets tricky: Sometimes the "how" only shows up on a need-to-know basis, and this is where people, and skeptics, get stuck. If the "how" isn't immediately available, you will often hear the immediate excuse of "I can't see how that would work, so therefore it cannot be so." It is the age-old struggle the paranormal has wrestled since the first reports of strange phenomena. The "how" is not always present, but it doesn't make the phenomena any less apparent. The photos still exist, the lab results are still there, and the evidence can still be replicated. Sometimes the "how" isn't ready, and there are times we simply aren't ready for it. Remember, we get what we believe is possible, not what we want.

Don't wait for the "how." This is where instinct and faith become the most reliable friends in your court. Trust the "how" will make itself known, because it will and does. The steps show up and unfold grander than you ever thought possible.

Many times, people get hung up on the letting go. The ability to be still within yourself, to prepare the mind and the environment for the arrival of what's coming is crucial. Stillness is key in most psi experiments, and *inner* stillness is most important. It is the ability to listen for the instruction instead of begging for direction. The paranormal is a teacher in forcing us to look inwards, because in order to experience it the way we were meant to, we have to be in touch with the part of who we are that often gets ignored and pushed aside. Stillness and being alright with sitting with our Selves is such a large part of the process that it can't be ignored. This is a struggle for many people, and maybe it's a struggle for you. Maybe you have a million projects on the go just so you don't have to stop and sit with your Self, or maybe you drown it out with drama or addiction. It comes in many forms. But the question we must ask ourselves is "Are we giving room for the instruction?" Most of us are not! It's one of the top reasons people who want to have a spiritual experience don't have one! You want to have a connection with your dear and beloved dead grandmother, but have you left space in your life for that communication? Are you complaining and noticing you don't have it, or are you listening? How much time do you spend noticing she's not there rather than expecting an answer?

Part of being still is learning how to be authentic, to speak your truth with integrity. Integrity is what happens when what you think, feel and do are all in alignment with the greater part of who you are. When one of those are out of line, you're out of order, and you've got to clean that up. Ask yourself: is what you think, feel, and do (including what you speak) in alignment with your vision? I will put five bucks on the notion that if you don't have what you want in life, one of these points may well be out of order. If you want to be rich, but you're complaining about an empty bank account, you've got a problem. If you want frightening phenomena to stop plaguing your household, you've got to stop talking about it to your friends and start telling a different story. How you follow up the words "I Am" *matters* (yes, that's a capital *A*). Neville Goddard felt that the "I Am" was the embodiment of a Creator spirit. Whatever you follow "I Am" with determines your state of being and your story. Don't tolerate what doesn't honor you, whether it's coming out of your mouth or your actions or someone else's. Call it out and be your own best friend. Ask yourself and others the hard questions because your vision, your creations, your joy depends on *you*.

Spiritual teacher Iyanla Vanzant once said: "If you don't love what you're doing, run for your life." It's one of the most profound statements you will likely take from this book because it embodies the lessons of so many of the parapsychologists, neurologists, philosophers and researchers whom we have already discussed. Each one had to find that path for themselves, but every one of them, you may have noticed, has a similar story. There is a thread that runs through all of them, and while how they got there may have differed greatly, the path to carving out their own journey and understanding eventually turns us inward. Psi research has a way of causing us to pay attention to our own vision because when you get to the bare bones of this research, you cannot help but ask yourself what it is you can want and achieve in this physical life. Each one was willing to do the thing that scared them: leave their job, put reputations on the line, risk ridicule, try new things, and be daring enough to think outside the normal box when they were dreaming of what they really could accomplish. With many, it began as a question that seems external: What is psi? What is the paranormal phenomena I'm witnessing? Following that calling led them so much deeper, as a good vision must. They were willing to go one step further than just standing in someone else's light, they were willing to dream of owning the building with the light in it! But owning the building takes a lot more than just stepping into the light someone else's vision provides for you. There are risks, there is doubt, there are naysayers who will try to tear down everything your instinct tells you is there. The dreams and knowledge that exist in what Eben Alexander called "the Core" and the faith it can require to get from having the vision of what you want, not seeing it in the physical in any way, shape or form, and then having it expand into the empirical world requires discipline.

Trailblazers move by instinct and faith. It doesn't matter what field you're in. It doesn't always look rational or logical, especially in parapsychology, as sometimes we have to question the very order of matter in attempts to explain the results before our very eyes. There doesn't have to be a precedent in order for you to succeed. Just because it has never been done before or it may seem as if that vision is beyond any current understanding doesn't mean it is any less valid. What I have discovered is if the universe or consciousness has inspired it in you, it has the ability to follow it through. However, it will come through you, not to you, and much of that step lies in the preparation period.

Your talents will bring you to a place, and in order to understand and to show up for your vision in a meaningful way, you have to understand why you're there. So many people arrive someplace and have no idea how to answer that question: Why are you there? What are you bringing to the table? Where have your talents and journey taken you? Understanding why and how you're showing up to your vision will keep your instinct clear and will keep you on the path when the people around you tell you you're crazy as hell! For some people, not even the best or most qualitative evidence will be enough if they have a paradigm set in their mind that something cannot be done and,

MORGAN KNUDSEN

because of the laws of the universe, the results *they* get will prove to them it cannot. You get what you believe about.

You also cannot do this alone. There are times you will *be* alone, but those preparation periods are about *you*, not about them. Your moais will show up when you get clear about where you're headed; the right people will become interested. The movers, the shakers, the door openers will arrive based on your own point of attraction, which depends on the factors we've been talking about throughout this book. Your vision is a living, breathing, swirling manifestation that will gather to it the components needed and the direction required to move you to things and through things you can only begin to imagine, if you let it. When those who do not understand or try to talk you out of what you've got going on, let them go. They don't have to agree with you. We didn't come, as energetic, powerful creators on this planet, to convince others or justify to them. We came to be, do and have a vision for our life that makes us wake up in the morning knowing there is something more than going to a job we hate to pay bills in a house we're never in. For some people, it takes a near-death experience and severe meningitis to figure things out, but with any hope you will put this book down and see a glimmer of that magic for yourself. Others did it, have done it, are doing it, and so can you.

Now, *what do you want?*

CONCLUSION

Here we are. My hope and intention is that you read this book and are left with questions. Questions, of course, about what's "out there," but also questions about what's "in here." Parapsychology has been a study that has been glossed over, dismissed, berated, and bastardized throughout the years for many reasons and on many platforms, but the questions it is attempting to answer are some of the greatest mankind has asked. Who are we? Not just as physical humans, but who are we really? The question terrifies many because understanding the power of our true nature as people on any level can place a level of responsibility on us that many simply don't want. Many have a hard enough time trying to manage the matter around them let alone conceive of anything existing in nonphysical. But the truth is we already deal with what we can't see on a daily basis: gravity, illnesses, infrasound, air and wind, and other constants in our environment we have learned

215

to understand and live with. The question becomes now: are we willing to take a grander, less limited approach to that which we are as conscious beings, *and* are we brave enough for the answers? Those are two very different problems.

My hope is that, after reading this, you begin to see yourself differently, that you begin to see instinct as a gift that can be honed, nurtured, and as a potential connection to something greater than you. Instinct is a gift, and the only way to tap into that gift is to stop putting limitations on the mind and realize it is a small piece, a clue, into the true capabilities of human consciousness. It is the inkling that tells us there is more to us than what we have been taught to believe, and it is what calls us forward into dreams, out of danger, and towards what we truly desire. It can be the subtle feeling of something being "off," or it can be the river of passion for something that calls you higher. It can bring you to places and people that can take us to new heights and cause us to avoid the ones who will kill our spirit. Instinct is a calling. It will move you, take care of you, nurture you, guide you, lead you, and most of all, it will cause you to *hear*. It will teach you about energy, about vibration, and about a language that has no speech. Instinct is there for us to lean into when there is no one around us who has direction. It teaches us to be still, to follow our calling, and will bring us, inevitably, to new understanding. This is the space between thought and the silence between words; it is the stillness, yet it is forever alive and steady. It is our built-in guidance consciousness uses to connect with the thinking and feeling part of our humanness. You have it for a reason, and if you elevate it enough, it can be a doorway to your peace, love and purpose.

Use it well.

REFERENCES

Schwartz, S. (2017). "Remote Viewing." *Psi Encyclopedia*. London: The Society for Psychical Research. <https://psi-encyclopedia.spr.ac.uk/articles/remote-viewing>. Retrieved 26 November 2021.

Rhine Feather, S. and Ensrud, B. (2018). "J. B. Rhine." *Psi Encyclopedia*. London: The Society for Psychical Research. <https://psi-encyclopedia.spr.ac.uk/articles/jb-rhine>. Retrieved 27 November 2021.

Roney-Dougal, S. (2015). "Meditation and Psi." *Psi Encyclopedia*. London: The Society for Psychical Research. <https://psi-encyclopedia.spr.ac.uk/articles/meditation-and-psi>. Retrieved 1 December 2021.

Puhle, A. (2017). "Extraordinary Light Phenomena." *Psi Encyclopedia*. London: The Society for Psychical Research.

<https://psi-encyclopedia.spr.ac.uk/articles/extraordinary-light-phenomena>. Retrieved 12 December 2021.

Wehrstein, KM (2018). "Eben Alexander." *Psi Encyclopedia*. London: The Society for Psychical Research. <https://psi-encyclopedia.spr.ac.uk/articles/eben-alexander>. Retrieved 12 December 2021.

Sartori, P. (2015). "Near-Death Experience." *Psi Encyclopedia*. London: The Society for Psychical Research. <https://psi-encyclopedia.spr.ac.uk/articles/near-death-experience>. Retrieved 13 December 2021.

Duggan, M. (2020). "Callum E Cooper." *Psi Encyclopedia*. London: The Society for Psychical Research. <https://psi-encyclopedia.spr.ac.uk/articles/callum-e-cooper>. Retrieved 13 December 2021.

Matlock, J. G (2021). "Eileen J Garrett." *Psi Encyclopedia*. London: The Society for Psychical Research. <https://psi-encyclopedia.spr.ac.uk/articles/eileen-j-garrett>. Retrieved 17 December 2021.

Willin, M. (2015). "The Enfield Poltergeist." *Psi Encyclopedia*. London: The Society for Psychical Research. <https://psi-encyclopedia.spr.ac.uk/articles/enfield-poltergeist>. Retrieved 7 January 2022.

Willin, M. (2021). "Maurice Grosse." *Psi Encyclopedia*. London: The Society for Psychical Research. <https://psi-encyclopedia.spr.ac.uk/articles/maurice-grosse>. Retrieved 7 January 2022.

Playfair, Guy Lyon & Grosse, Maurice, (1989). "Enfield Revisited: the evaporation of positive evidence." *Journal of the Society for Psychical Research* 55, pp. 208–19.

"Report of the Enfield Poltergeist Investigation Committee." SPR Archive. Cambridge University Library.

Maurice Grosse, The Paranormal Review, Issue 24, October 2002, "After 120 Years Of Psychical Research – Confusion Abounds!" p. 9)

Wehrstein, KM (2019). "William Roll." *Psi Encyclopedia*. London: The Society for Psychical Research. <https://psi-encyclopedia.spr.ac.uk/articles/william-roll>. Retrieved 29 January 2022.

Duggan, M. (2018). "Ingo Swann." *Psi Encyclopedia*. London: The Society for Psychical Research. <https://psi-encyclopedia.spr.ac.uk/articles/ingo-swann>. Retrieved 29 January 2022.

Duggan, M. (2017). "Psychokinesis Research." *Psi Encyclopedia*. London: The Society for Psychical Research. <https://psi-encyclopedia.spr.ac.uk/articles/psychokinesis-research>. Retrieved 30 January 2022.

Williams, B. (2019). "Psychological Aspects in Poltergeist Cases." *Psi Encyclopedia*. London: The Society for Psychical Research. <https://psi-encyclopedia.spr.ac.uk/articles/psychological-aspects-poltergeist-cases>. Retrieved 30 January 2022.

The Poltergeist (1972). New York: N Doubleday.

Theory and Experiment in Psychical Research (1975). New York: Ayer. (MLitt thesis).

Psychic Connections: A Journey into the Mysterious World of Psi (1995). Co-authored with Lois Duncan. New York: Delacorte Books for Young Readers.

Unleashed. Of Poltergeists and Murder: The Curious Story of Tina Resch. (2004). *(With V. S*torey) New York: Paraview Pocket Books.

Roll, W.G. (2000). Poltergeist and Space-Time: A Contemplation on Hans Bender's Ideas About RSPK. *The Parapsychological Association, 43rd Annual Convention, Proceedings of Presented Papers*, August 17–20, 316–332.

Duggan, M. (2021). "Joe Gallenberger." *Psi Encyclopedia*. London: The Society for Psychical Research. <https://psi-encyclopedia.spr.ac.uk/articles/joe-gallenberger>. Retrieved 1 February 2022.

Moss, Charles. (2021). "Finally, The Truth Behind The 'Haunted' Dybbuk Box Can Be Revealed." Input Magazine.

<https://www.inputmag.com/features/dybbuk-box-dibbuk-kevin-mannis-zak-bagans-haunted-hoax-revealed>

Saunders, D. (2015). "Dreams and ESP." *Psi Encyclopedia.* London: The Society for Psychical Research. <https://psi-encyclopedia.spr.ac.uk/articles/dreams-and-esp>. Retrieved 16 February 2022.

Horowitz, Mitch. (2016). "Neville Goddard: A Cosmic Philosopher." HarvBishop.com. https://www.harvbishop.com/neville-goddard-a-cosmic-philospher/

ABOUT THE AUTHOR

Award-winning co-founder of Entityseeker Paranormal Research, Investigations & Teachings, as well as the world-renowned Teaching the Living program for clients, Morgan Knudsen brings classes and presentations on this phenomenon to a new level. With inspiring lectures that include fire art demonstrations, mind-blowing evidence, and uplifting stories, Morgan makes audiences recognize that managing who they are on the inside directly impacts what they experience on the outside, and to re-examine the world they thought they knew.

Co-founding and leading **Entityseeker Paranormal Research & Teachings** since 2003, her experiences and knowledge have led to researching and co-creating a unique investigative program called **Teaching the Living,** and subsequently she has been featured on and hosted numerous specials and TV shows (**The Discovery Channel, "A Haunting", T+E, Destination America, The Travel Channel, CBC, CTV, Planete+, TLC, Crime + Investigation, Celestial Tiger** networks in China, and **COAST TO COAST AM**). Morgan uses her outgoing, tell-it-like-it-is approach in determining haunted locations and creating solutions for the people involved. Her programs are now practiced in three different countries and a part of numerous social work and psychology secondary education courses in Canada. Morgan subsequently received the award from the **City of Edmonton for Outstanding Service in 2008** and graduated from **The AZIRE: The Alvarado Zingrone Institute for Research and Education** two years in a row, receiving two graduating **Certificates of Distinction** in parapsychology. Morgan is also a regular contributor to the number one magazine in the UK, **HAUNTED MAGAZINE.** Her work has been presented at the **Rhine Research Institute**, and she has been a featured presenter at the **Parapsychological Association**. Her book *Teaching the Living: Heartbreak to Happiness in a Haunted Home* is now available.

Morgan can also be heard on her podcast, **SUPERNATURAL CIRCUMSTANCES**, with co-host/co-creator Mike

Browne (Dark Poutine), which delves into the mysterious, the spiritual, and the fascinating things in our universe.

MORGAN KNUDSEN
OFFICIAL SITE: www.entityseeker.ca
FACEBOOK: facebook.com/entityseeker
TWITTER: @MorganKnudsen

SUPERNATURAL CIRCUMSTANCES Podcast
OFFICIAL SITE: www.supernaturalcircumstances.com
FACEBOOK: facebook.com/supernaturalcircumstances
TWITTER: @SupernaturalPC

PREVIOUS WORKS:
Teaching the Living: From Heartbreak to Happiness in a Haunted Home (2021)

Teaching The Living: From Heartbreak to Happiness in a Haunted Home

Made in the USA
Middletown, DE
29 May 2022

66360456R00149